CRITICAL ETHNOGRAPHIC PERSPECTIVES ON MEDICAL TRAVEL

By taking an ethnographic approach to medical travel, this important book uses critical perspectives to understand inequalities in healthcare access and delivery, including gender, class and ethnicity, and explores how these are negotiated. In this key text Vindrola-Padros presents a comprehensive overview of the work carried out on this topic to date, highlights the gaps that remain and suggests strategies for enriching medical travel research in the future.

Drawing from the author's research on internal medical travel to access pediatric oncology treatment in Buenos Aires, Argentina and other research from across the globe, this book presents three dimensions of medical travel that can be explored through a critical (im)mobilities lens: infrastructures, differential mobility empowerments, and affective dimensions of care and travel. Vindrola-Padros encourages the reader to critically explore processes of medical travel by considering the structures that shape travel, individual capacities for travel, the role emotions play in decisions and experiences of movement and service delivery, and the ways in which culture(s) influence both travel and care.

This book will be important reading for scholars across medical sociology, anthropology and critical health studies.

CECILIA VINDROLA-PADROS is a medical anthropologist working at University College London. Her research focuses on topics such as: embedded research, rapid qualitative research, health service reconfigurations, and the delivery of complex treatment in LMICs. She is interested in the relationship between mobility and health and has carried out research on medical travel for over ten years.

Critical Approaches to Health

The Routledge *Critical Approaches to Health* series aims to present critical, inter-disciplinary books around psychological, social and cultural issues related to health. Each volume in the series provides a critical approach to a particular issue or important topic, and is of interest and relevance to students and practitioners across the social sciences. The series is produced in association with the International Society of Critical Health Psychology (ISCHP).

Series Editors: Kerry Chamberlain & Antonia Lyons

Titles in the series:

Disability and Sexual Health
Critical Psychological Perspectives
Poul Rohleder, Stine Hellum Braathen and Mark T. Carew

Postfeminism and Health
Critical Psychology and Media Perspectives
Sarah Riley, Adrienne Evans, and Martine Robson

Health at Work
Critical Perspectives
Leah Tomkins and Katrina Pritchard

For more information about this series, please visit: www.routledge.com/ Critical-Approaches-to-Health/book-series/CRITHEA

CRITICAL ETHNOGRAPHIC PERSPECTIVES ON MEDICAL TRAVEL

Cecilia Vindrola-Padros

First published 2020
by Routledge
2 Park Square, Milton Park, Abingdon, Oxon OX14 4RN

and by Routledge
52 Vanderbilt Avenue, New York, NY 10017

Routledge is an imprint of the Taylor & Francis Group, an informa business

© 2020 Cecilia Vindrola-Padros

The right of Cecilia Vindrola-Padros to be identified as author of this work has been asserted by her in accordance with sections 77 and 78 of the Copyright, Designs and Patents Act 1988.

All rights reserved. No part of this book may be reprinted or reproduced or utilised in any form or by any electronic, mechanical, or other means, now known or hereafter invented, including photocopying and recording, or in any information storage or retrieval system, without permission in writing from the publishers.

Trademark notice: Product or corporate names may be trademarks or registered trademarks, and are used only for identification and explanation without intent to infringe.

British Library Cataloguing-in-Publication Data
A catalogue record for this book is available from the British Library

Library of Congress Cataloging-in-Publication Data
A catalog record has been requested for this book

ISBN: 978-0-815-38525-7 (hbk)
ISBN: 978-0-367-37159-3 (pbk)
ISBN: 978-1-351-20203-9 (ebk)

Typeset in Minion Pro
by Newgen Publishing UK

 Printed in the United Kingdom by Henry Ling Limited

To my parents, for teaching me to
question <u>everything</u>.

CONTENTS

Series editor preface   ix

CHAPTER 1   INTRODUCTION   1

CHAPTER 2   CRITICAL PERSPECTIVES ON MEDICAL TRAVEL   17

CHAPTER 3   MEDICAL TRAVEL AT A GLOBAL SCALE   37

CHAPTER 4   MEDICAL TRAVEL AT A LOCAL SCALE: AN EXAMPLE OF INTRA-NATIONAL MEDICAL TRAVEL   57

CHAPTER 5   MEDICAL TRAVEL INFRASTRUCTURES   83

CHAPTER 6   DIFFERENTIAL MEDICAL TRAVEL EXPERIENCES AND POSSIBILITIES   95

CHAPTER 7   AFFECTIVE JOURNEYS AND THE IMAGINATION   113

CHAPTER 8   FUTURE DIRECTIONS IN MEDICAL TRAVEL RESEARCH   123

Bibliography   *131*
Index   *155*

SERIES EDITOR PREFACE

CRITICAL APPROACHES TO HEALTH

Health is a major issue for people all around the world, and is fundamental to individual well-being, personal achievements and satisfaction, as well as to families, communities and societies. It is also embedded in social notions of participation and citizenship. Much has been written about health, from a variety of perspectives and disciplines, but a lot of this writing takes a biomedical and causally positivist approach to health matters, neglecting the historical, social, and cultural contexts and environments within which health is experienced, understood, and practiced. It is timely for a new series of books that offer critical, social science perspectives on important health topics.

The Critical Approaches to Health series aims to provide new critical writing on health by presenting critical, interdisciplinary, and theoretical writing about health, where matters of health are framed quite broadly. The series seeks to include books that range across important health matters, including general health-related issues (such as gender and media), major social issues for health (such as medicalization, obesity, and palliative care), particular health concerns (such as pain, doctor-patient interaction, health services, and health technologies), particular health problems (such as diabetes, autoimmune disease, and medically unexplained illness), or health for specific groups of people (such as the health of migrants, the homeless, and the aged), or combinations of these.

The series seeks above all to promote critical thought about health matters. By critical, we mean going beyond the critique of the topic and work in the field, to more general considerations of power and benefit, and in particular, to addressing concerns about whose understandings and interests are upheld and whose are marginalized by the approaches, findings, and practices in these various domains of health. Such critical agendas involve reflections on what constitutes knowledge, how it is created, and how it is used. Accordingly, critical approaches consider epistemological and theoretical positioning, as well as issues of methodology and practice, and seek to examine how health is enmeshed within broader social relations and structures. Books within this series take up this challenge and seek to provide new insights and understandings by applying a critical agenda to their topics.

In this book, *Critical Ethnographic Perspectives on Medical Travel*, Cecilia Vindrola-Padros discusses an increasingly important health issue, namely travel to obtain healthcare and services, and provides a critical mobilities theoretical framework to the research in this field. She examines the scope and intent of travel for healthcare, and how such travel can both assist and constrain local healthcare and services. Vindrola-Padros documents how medical travel is a global industry worth billions of dollars and affects most healthcare systems across the world. She examines medical travel at both the global and local levels, bringing together the wide variety of health and medical travel that takes place across the globe. This covers travel by people to other countries, and by immigrants returning to their countries of origin, to gain access to better quality services, more culturally appropriate services, or services unavailable or illegal in the traveler's own country, as well as including travel within one's own country to gain access to scarce health resources. Vindrola-Padros considers not just the client/patient but also their families, networks, support people, and carers, particularly when children are involved. She highlights the diversity of reasons for medical travel, from seeking treatments that are unavailable in the local region (e.g. for cancer) to seeking procedures that are cheaper in other countries (e.g. plastic surgery).

The book critically examines the international research into the diversity of medical travel and is informed by case studies from the author's own research in this field. The book draws heavily on ethnographic research and offers a thoughtful discussion of critical perspectives for understanding medical travel, before arguing for the value of a critical mobilities theoretical perspective. This provides for an examination of medical travel from a variety of viewpoints, both practical and symbolic. Separate chapters examine healthcare infrastructures, the diversity of medical travel practices and experiences and inequalities in access to such travel, and the affective investment and care that such travel necessarily invokes. Throughout the book, Vindrola-Padros critically explores the various structures that shape and form medical travel, how travelers negotiate and experience these structures, how emotions and imaginations have a role in creating and enacting medical travel, and how inequality is implicated in both medical travel and the provision of service delivery and care.

The book successfully highlights the diversity and complexity of medical travel, and the people that undertake it, documenting how their experiences are shaped by location, resources, (im)mobility, imagination, emotion, and the structuring of services and care. In the final chapter, Vindrola-Padros offers some recommendations for the direction of future research in this fascinating field, for as she argues "As more and more people travel to obtain care far from home, a critical analysis of medical travel becomes even more relevant." This book offers a very timely consideration of the medical travel phenomenon.

Kerry Chamberlain & Antonia Lyons, June 2019

# CHAPTER ONE
Introduction

INTRODUCTION

> *"The doctor knows we always come back. This is why he lets us go home in between treatments. We are never late for an appointment. We get up at three in the morning to walk to the bus stop for our first bus. One time we overslept and had to run to the stop, but we did not miss our bus. We ride this bus for about an hour. It takes us to a big bus station where we wait for our second one. We normally have to wait about one hour. This bus trip is longer, about two hours. We then get to the city. We try to take the metro, but it depends on how full it is. We normally take a third bus for about 40 minutes. This one leaves us close to the hospital. We walk about 20 minutes and we are there. Once we get to the hospital, we need to wait in line to queue for our appointment. Last time, we stood in line for three hours, but we were able to see the doctor. When we are done, it is the same thing all over again, the buses, the waiting, all until we are able to get home again. We always come back for the treatment, though, she ... [points to her five-year-old child] would die without it."*
>
> (Eulalia, mother traveling for care for her ill child, Argentina, 2010)

Approximately five million people travel each year to obtain medical care abroad (Horsfall & Lunt, 2016). These travels are highly publicized as we hear about rich North Americans who travel to Brazil or Costa Rica for cosmetic surgery or Eastern Europe for in-vitro fertilization (IVF). This figure of five million people is misleading as not all countries have mechanisms for reporting the number of foreign patients receiving treatment (Whittaker, 2010). Furthermore, it does not consider patients traveling within regions or countries, pointing to a potential higher number of people seeking care away from their place of residence.

The process of traveling to obtain medical services in another location is often referred to as medical travel (Sobo, 2011). People decide to engage in medical travel to obtain cheaper or quicker services, access treatments not available (or legal) near their home, to obtain higher quality of care, more culturally appropriate care, or because they do not trust local services (Agee et al., 2006; Knodel et al., 2003; Vindrola-Padros & Johnson, 2015). Patients will travel to far away countries, cross nearby borders, travel within their country or region or return to their home country for care (Inhorn, 2015;

Speier, 2016). Medical travel has become a global industry worth billions of dollars and currently affects most healthcare systems across the world.

Promoters of medical travel have argued that some aspects of this type of industry can generate financial profit for the host hospital which then spills over into the public health sector, improving the lives of the lowest social classes (Hopkins et al., 2010; Helble, 2011). As argued by political leaders and medical travel supporters, medical travel has the potential to make a contribution to the development of health services, giving local healthcare professionals access to specialized training and making new specialties and technologies available to the local population (Hopkins et al., 2010; Snyder et al., 2013). Income obtained by offering medical treatment to foreign patients (treatment-based income as well as income obtained from hospitality services) can then be invested in other sectors of the host country that require additional funding such as social services or education (Chen & Flood, 2013). Under this logic, the benefits of medical travel "trickle down" to all areas of society (Chen & Flood, 2013).

Current research has indicated that the movement of patients opens opportunities to new forms of healthcare or higher quality of services for some populations, but limits access to care for others (Chen & Flood, 2013; Whittaker et al., 2010). Not everyone who needs or wants to travel to another location will be able to do so. Healthcare systems are not always equipped to deal with incoming patients as well as the loss of patients who seek services elsewhere (Chen & Flood, 2013; Kassim, 2009). Medical travel destinations often create two-tiered health systems, offering incoming patients new medical technologies and specialized personnel, and forcing local populations to pay for services or only giving them access to low quality services (Alsharif et al., 2010; Helble, 2011).

Previous research has indicated that medical travel tends to escalate the cost of healthcare for local populations (Saniotis, 2007), draws scarce resources such as capital, technology, and personnel from public medical facilities (Chen & Flood, 2013), and shifts the allocation of resources from primary to tertiary care (Alsharif et al., 2010; Smith et al., 2011). The quality of care available to medical travelers is not the same as that offered to local patients, as medical tourists can afford to pay for personalized attention, senior-level clinical staff, and luxurious hospital rooms (Chen & Flood, 2013). Medical travel can often lead to brain drain as healthcare professionals from rural areas relocate to urban areas, and, at a global scale, those from low- and middle-income countries (LMICs) migrate to high-income countries (HICs) (Plotnikova, 2018). The private facilities that provide care to medical travelers tend to be more attractive to healthcare professionals as the salaries are higher, working hours are shorter, and the working environment is better (Chen & Flood, 2013). As a result, brain drain leaves considerable areas of LMICs with a reduced number of healthcare professionals, increasing the number of people per professional and leading to the overworking of staff in public hospitals and primary care. In sum, a global overview of medical travel points to evident inequalities in the distribution of high-quality medical services that need to be taken into consideration.

The aim of this book is to bring the analysis of these inequalities to the forefront of studies of medical travel. It seeks to achieve this aim by drawing from critical perspectives such as critical medical anthropology (CMA), critical geography, critical ethics, post-colonial theory and the critical (im)mobilities framework, which explore how processes of care and illness are shaped by local and global political economies. The book argues that the combination of critical theory and the mobilities paradigm can open new avenues of exploration in the field of medical travel. The mobilities paradigm visualizes social life as the production of constant flows of people, ideas, and objects (Urry, 2007). This paradigm presented a recent shift in the social sciences, where mobilities are studied in their own singularity and centrality and not as a result of studying other phenomena (D'Andrea et al., 2011). This shift entailed reconceptualizing processes that had up until then been studied as static or sedentary, and developing terminology to account for a renewed focus on movement (Urry, 2002). It also meant exploring a wide range of mobility forms and the factors that promoted or hindered movement (Salazar et al., 2017).

The variability in the willingness and capacity to move became the focus of authors interested in integrating critical perspectives to the 'mobilities paradigm' (Cresswell, 2011; Hannam et al., 2006). A critical (im)mobilities framework was developed to account for the role of asymmetries in power in the shaping of episodes of movement and stasis (Soderström et al., 2013). In other words, it sought to identify the structures that allow some to move, while preventing others from doing so. This framework has also focused on exploring how factors such as class, gender, and ethnicity contribute to the creation of particular types of movement or experiences of staying still. It has also engaged with inequalities operating at symbolic levels, such as emotions and the imagination, where we do not all have the same imagined possibilities and the emotions we experience through travel might range from excitement and enchantment to frustration and fear.

In sum, the critical (im)mobilities framework explores the creation and reproduction of inequalities in experiences and perceptions of movement, considering both the structures that shape these as well as the ways in which these structures are negotiated by social actors. Why is this framework relevant and useful for studies of medical travel? As discussed earlier, medical travel is embedded in wider political and economic processes operating at a global scale, where not all healthcare systems have the same level of development and some patients have access to high-quality care at the sake of others. This framework can explore how these global processes are negotiated and reconfigured by individuals on a daily basis, as patients seeking medical services away from their place of origin must often bypass deficiencies in services and other barriers to care.

A critical (im)mobilities framework can also give us tools to unpack medical travel as a concept, questioning what we mean by medical (i.e. Is it only biomedical services we are referring to? Are we including other forms of care intimately connected to biomedicine?) and travel (i.e. Should we only look at international travel? What about other forms of more localized movement? Should we consider who travels and with whom?). This process of deconstruction inevitably points to the wide range of mobility forms involved in medical travel as well as experiences and perceptions of both travel and care. This brings us to a much-needed discussion of terminology.

TERMINOLOGY

A considerable amount of research has studied medical travel under the concept of 'medical tourism,' a term that alludes to the temporal, elective, one-time, and potentially 'worry-free' nature of medical travel

(Kangas, 2011; Sobo et al., 2011). It also positions patients as consumers and tends to focus primarily on the need to cross national borders to obtain care (Lunt et al., 2014). An in-depth exploration of medical travel experiences across the globe, however, points to the complex and difficult realities faced by many patients who need to seek care away from home, the loss of employment, financial difficulties, feelings of homesickness, and family separation that the need to travel for treatment demands (Kangas, 2007; Vindrola-Padros & Brage, 2017). Medical travel has been proposed as a more 'value-free' way of thinking about and studying this type of travel (Sobo, 2011).

Some authors have called for greater specificity, proposing terms such as cross-border care to identify cases of travel between bordering countries and return migration to describe travel of individuals who return to their place of origin to access care (Inhorn, 2011; Whittaker & Speier, 2010). Others have opted for more encompassing terms such as assistance migration (mainly found in publications in Spanish) to highlight the fact that individuals will travel for medical services, but will often need other non-medical services as well (i.e. support with temporary housing or funding from the government to cover travel costs) (ROHA, 2008).

Another trend in research has been to move beyond 'value-free' concepts and work with terminology to respond to the political economies of healthcare, highlighting the relationship between lack of access to medical services close to home and the need to travel to access these services elsewhere and the impossibility of the nation-state to provide the care needed by its citizens (Ormond, 2015a). The terms "medical exile" and "medical refugees" have been proposed to allude to this situation (Inhorn, 2011; Ormond, 2013). "Biomedical pilgrimage" has been proposed by Song (2010), to underscore the cultural and symbolic dimensions of medical travel, journeys that might acquire religious or spiritual connotations.

An important issue to consider, is the idea attached to the term. For instance, the term medical travel is widely used in the literature and accepted as the best way to address the different types of journeys that might be carried out to access medical services. Yet, this term is normally used to refer to international travel, leaving the experiences of individuals who travel within their countries to access care largely unexplored. The neglect of these internal medical travel experiences overlooks the hardship and complexity of these journeys (Vindrola-Padros & Johnson, 2015; Vindrola-Padros & Brage, 2017).

In this book, medical travel is defined as any type of travel performed to obtain medical care. This includes international and intra-national journeys, one-time trips as well as regular forms of travel. This broader conceptualization of medical travel recognizes that all journeys designed with the purpose of obtaining care are important, have meaning, and have their own requirements and connotations. In considering the diversity of mobility forms associated with seeking care elsewhere, this concept of medical travel attempts to grasp the nuances of how treatments, medical spaces, and experiences of care are made and unmade through movement.

The focus on different mobility forms points to the wide range of simultaneous and often overlapping journeys of patients, each with its own characteristics, ranging from, for instance, patients who travel for cosmetic procedures to those traveling with the desperation to save their life (Connell, 2006). In addition to the reason for travel, the way in which travel is performed also varies, from the patient who travels by plane to be picked up at an airport and taken to the hotel where they will await their procedure, to those traveling thousands of kilometers using buses to reach a strange city where they will have to find their own way to the hospital (as in Eulalia's story above).

These journeys are enacted by people with complex feelings and histories that need to be recognized. In this book, I use the term 'patient' to refer to individuals seeking care. The limitations of using 'patient' have been rehearsed in the literature. 'Patient' tends to objectify, represent a passive, perhaps submissive, inclination to healthcare delivery and depict a homogenous group of people (van der Geest & Finkler, 2004). My decision to use the term patient is solely based on ensuring clarity and distinguishing those receiving care from those accompanying them or delivering care. I hope the rich descriptions of individuals' agency in the text and the detailed description of their stories moves beyond homogeneous and static representations of 'the patient' that have been previously critiqued.

INTRODUCTION

STUDIES OF MEDICAL TRAVEL

Early studies of medical travel have emerged from clinical fields such as medicine and nursing, exploring the potential consequences of patients seeking care abroad. Medical travel was explored from a legal and ethical point of view and authors tended to highlight issues around global regulation of care, malpractice, and dealing with complications when patients returned to their place of origin (Burkett, 2007; Hunter & Oultram, 2010; Martin, 2010; Parks, 2010; Pennings, 2004; Storrow, 2005). The main patient flows explored by this literature were those of US or European patients seeking elective care in the Global South, and most of these journeys were explored from a macro-level point of view, without focusing on patients' experiences of care.

A later trend in medical travel research took an empirical turn as it became preoccupied with the generation of data on patient numbers, experiences of care, and descriptions of the ways in which care is delivered to foreign patients (Lunt et al., 2015). International travel was still the main focus, but there was an increase in the research focusing on intra-regional travel and cross-border care (Ormond, 2013, 2015b; Inhorn, 2007). Several literature reviews were developed, mainly exploring the information provided by medical travel facilitators (Cormany & Baloglu, 2011), the impact of medical travel (Johnston et al., 2010), and the state of existing knowledge on medical travel (Hopkins et al., 2010; Lunt & Carrera, 2010; Smith et al., 2011).

Although medical travel has been explored through various lenses stemming from different disciplines, the approach that has generated the richest and most nuanced interpretations of medical travel experiences has been ethnographic research (Sobo, 2011). Ethnographic research has been defined as an approach that seeks to understand the world through the eyes and experiences of others, recognizing the important role contextual factors play in the shaping of this world-vision and experience (Le Compte & Schensul, 2013). It considers the highly mediated nature of this interpretation of the lives of others, through the ethnographer's own life experience and theoretical inclinations (Pink et al., 2004). The descriptions and interpretations that make up the ethnographic text are, therefore, a collaborative creation between those we study and the ethnographer herself.

INTRODUCTION

As such, it has been identified as a fruitful mechanism through which to explore the processes of medical travel as well as the experiences of those receiving and delivering care. Ethnographies of medical travel have highlighted the multi-directionality of patient flows due to their focus on micro, meso, and macro scales of research and coverage of the different areas where medical travel occurs (from individuals seeking care to the global medical travel market) (Kangas, 2010; Sobo, 2009). The conceptual flexibility and methodological dynamism has allowed ethnographers to capture the production and reproduction of medical travel spaces, processes, and practices, highlighting how these change through time and how they might take on particular forms depending on those involved (for instance, the use of the same medical facilities for private and non-private patients). This multi-scalar view has also captured the unequal playing fields that characterize medical travel, with different levels of access to care and mobility (Kangas, 2010; Whittaker et al., 2010). Ethnographic approximations of medical travel have engaged with imaginaries, emotions, and other symbolic aspects of medical care and travel, the feelings of hope, solace, excitement, and desperation that emerge under the potential opportunity of finding a cure for a disease (Kangas, 2007; Parkin, 2014; Speier, 2011; Whittaker & Speier, 2010), and the emotional burden and carework associated with traveling patients (Ackerman, 2010).

Several ethnographies have been carried out on medical travel, covering topics such as travel for cosmetic surgery (Ackerman, 2010) and gender reassignment surgery (Aizura, 2010), assisted reproductive technologies (Bergmann, 2011a, 2011b; Inhorn, 1996, 2003, 2007, 2015; Speier, 2011, 2016; Whittaker, 2008), stem cell therapies (Song, 2010), and pediatric oncology treatment (Brage, 2018; Vindrola-Padros, 2011, 2012). These ethnographies have explored care delivery in various geographical contexts, including countries in the Middle East, Asia, Europe, and Latin America. Although most represent examples of international medical travel, some nod at the possibility of more regional or localized forms of travel and two ethnographies have focused solely on intra-national travel (Brage, 2018; Vindrola-Padros, 2011).

There is still considerable work to be done in our exploration of medical travel. Lunt and colleagues (2015) have called for the development of more theoretically-informed research. I concur with the authors and would argue that this theoretical invigoration should be accompanied by a wider exploration of medical travel, beyond international travel, to account for a wider range of regional and local forms of travel, including intra-national travel.

MY RESEARCH ON INTRA-NATIONAL MEDICAL TRAVEL

I have been studying intra-national medical travel in Argentina for over ten years. The centralized model of care delivery in this country, where most specialist centers are located in the capital of Buenos Aires, means that patients requiring specialized care often need to leave their place of origin to access medical services. This is particularly problematic in the case of complex and, sometimes, long-term medical treatments such as oncology treatment. My research has focused mainly on documenting the stories of children affected by cancer and their families, their journeys through different areas of the country before reaching Buenos Aires, how their experiences have changed over time, and the challenges they face on a daily basis while caring for ill children in a strained public health system and new city. This book is sprinkled with bits of this research to ground more abstract theoretical discussions in the lived realities of people seeking care away from home. The stories included in this book give color, flavor, and put a human face on processes of travel and accessing care.

WHY THIS BOOK?

This book seeks to examine processes of medical travel through the use of critical perspectives, and the critical (im)mobilities framework, in particular. As explained earlier, critical perspectives in health focus on inequalities in health outcomes, quality of life, and access to care (Scambler, 2013). The critical (im)mobilities framework seeks to examine different forms of movement and stasis as a way to gain insight into patterns of asymmetrical power and privilege (Soderström et al., 2013). One of the main arguments of this book is that the exploration of medical travel through the critical (im)mobilities lens will lead to the production of research capable of prioritizing the specificities of mobilities, rather than seeing them as incidences of a wider phenomenon. It will also provide a framework for the analysis of the power relations, structures, practices, and meanings that contribute to the (re)production of inequalities in medical travel and the delivery of care. A critical (im)mobilities framework will highlight the role played by imaginaries and emotions in processes of seeking and delivering care. Finally, it will shed light on a relatively unexplored area of research in studies of medical travel: the analysis of immobility, things that do not move, are stuck or fixed.

The book has three underlying themes, which correspond to the main dimensions of the critical (im)mobilities framework:

1. *Infrastructures*: The concept of infrastructures encompasses the roads, objects, networks, and institutions that can both facilitate and constrain movement (Urry, 2007; Korpela, 2016). It considers the structures and processes that need to be in place to (re)produce the flows of patients over time, but it is also flexible enough to account for improvisation and the individual's capacity to bypass barriers and create new infrastructures (Merriman, 2016). In the case of medical travel, it allows us to explore the wide range of actors involved in the creation and maintenance of medical travel processes, from the appropriation of tourism infrastructures for medical travel purposes to the emergence of medical travel facilitation companies and other types of brokers. The concept accounts for the role of informal actors (i.e. medical travelers who return home and convince others to seek care elsewhere) in the development of patient flows. It also acknowledges the fact that infrastructures change through time and can take on different characteristics and connotations depending on the context and individuals involved.
2. *Differential mobility empowerments*: The critical (im)mobilities framework recognizes that mobility is a process shaped by power relations. Not everyone who desires to move is able to do so and some people might be forced to move against their will (Morley, 2002; Skeggs, 2004). Mobility, then, is highly differentiated (Adey, 2006; Cresswell, 2011) and this differentiation is produced by the

performance of movement in social worlds that are shaped by politics, history, economics, and cultures. Individuals have, therefore, differential mobility empowerments, which, in the case of medical travel would urge us to unpack homogenous representations of medical travel and point to the diversity of medical travel practices and experiences. The focus on different levels of empowerment brings power relations to the forefront of analysis by acknowledging that not all who want to move are able to do so (or are able to move in the way they want to). This applies to actual movement as well as the journeys we imagine. Potential mobility, also referred to as motility (Kaufmann, 2002), is not evenly distributed, as our capacity to imagine and aspire is also socially constructed and context-dependent.

3. ***Affective (im)mobilities***: An important contribution of the mobilities turn was the recognition of the ways in which emotions, feelings, and the imagination permeate experiences of travel (Sherry & Urry, 2006). A critical (im)mobilities framework recognizes these symbolic dimensions of travel, but understands them in the context of prevailing social, political, and economic inequalities (Salazar, 2011). It explores how emotional responses are shaped by histories of exclusion, discrimination, or frustration, and uncovers how feelings of hope might only be triggered in those who see a potential capacity to travel, but would not be available to all.

STRUCTURE OF THE BOOK

The book is organized in eight chapters. This introduction represents Chapter 1 and here I have sought to provide an overview of the purpose and overall organization of the book. I introduce the reader to debates regarding the terminology used in medical travel studies and the main concepts that will appear throughout the book. I have also attempted to situate the book in the wider context of the medical travel literature. Chapter 2 provides an overview of some of the critical perspectives used in health services research, emphasizing the critical (im)mobilities framework. It introduces the reader to the mobilities turn in the social sciences and points to the ways in which our understanding and study of (im)mobilities changed. It then sets out a proposal for applying concepts from critical (im)mobilities to the study of medical travel.

Chapter 3 provides the reader with background on medical travel. It is designed as a 'catch-up' chapter for those not familiar with this field. It also includes an overview of the work carried out on medical travel so far, its main gaps and how this book seeks to address them. Chapter 4 presents an ethnographic case study of intra-national medical travel by discussing the findings from my own research on the experiences of families seeking pediatric oncology treatment in Argentina. It engages with the development of medical travel in Latin America, but highlights the particular healthcare context in Argentina, its longstanding history of the centralization of care and the relationship between this unequal distribution of services and flows of traveling patients. It introduces the reader to three stories of medical travel I encountered during fieldwork, grounding the discussions that take place later in the book.

Chapter 5 focuses on medical travel infrastructure, that is, the processes, structures, and practices that make medical travel possible for some, but not for others. The chapter looks at how national regulation of medical services contributes to the creation of medical travel industries. It explores the emergence of medical travel facilitators and brokers, the development of medical travel and tourism infrastructures in destination countries, and the role played by patient online communities in shaping the availability of services and success of medical travel companies.

The next chapter demonstrates the importance of studying the everydayness of health-seeking practices. By conceptualizing medical travel as a health-seeking practice, it is possible to see how individuals are able to play an active role in decisions about their health and healthcare (Hampshire et al., 2011). This chapter concentrates on delineating the diversity of medical travel forms by focusing on intra-national, regional, and local medical travel. The focus of this chapter is to represent travel as a social practice, thus highlighting the lived individual and collective meanings and motives to move and the ways in which these are negotiated on a daily basis (Manderscheid, 2014). It also considers mobility as a resource not available to all and explores how these inequalities play out in the search for medical treatment.

Chapter 7 explores the symbolic and imagined dimensions of medical travel. Significant work has been carried out in the mobilities literature to move beyond understanding travel as a purely physical act of movement, but instead consider the multiple forms of desired, imagined, or fantasized travel that might or might not happen (Lean et al., 2014; Leivestad, 2016; Salazar, 2013). Potential travel and unachieved travel are important to consider as they shed light on aspirations, which are themselves socially constructed (Leivestad, 2016; Salazar, 2011, 2013). These imaginaries will influence perceptions of care, decisions to travel, selections of destinations, and frame the journey as well as the experience in the new location (Aizura, 2010). The symbolic representations of medical travel will be imbued with affective dimensions, perhaps representing the journey as a source of desperation or hope (Kangas, 2007; Solomon, 2011). The destinations where medical travelers seek care are also instilled with feelings; these might be linked to ideas of "homeness" as in the case of migrants who seek treatment in their place of origin (Knodel & VanLandingham, 2003; Lee et al., 2010), or "exotic places" as in the case of medical travelers who seek care in locations far from home (Aizura, 2010). The chapter explores the relationships between health and culture and highlights the different ways in which medical travel is shaped by cultural factors. The chapter provides examples of the use of cultural features by destination countries, such as the use of strategic essentialism to underscore particular exotic qualities of the country to lure travelers.

Chapter 8 proposes the development of a medical travel research agenda based on the critical perspectives presented in previous chapters. The application of critical frameworks to the study of medical travel can allow us to see medical travel as a consequence of the unequal distribution of medical services, as well as a producer of inequalities. As researchers, we need to immerse ourselves in the daily lives of medical travelers and those who care for them, so we can examine movement across multiple locales and scales, in time, practice, and in the imagination (Dalakoglou & Harvey, 2012). Mobility can be theorized as a complex social process, entailing different modalities and layers of movement (Chalfin, 2016), and access to healthcare can be critically examined to uncover relations of power and structural inequalities that guarantee high-quality services for some and deny them for others (Willen et al., 2011).

INTRODUCTION

CONCLUDING THOUGHTS

Medical travel processes have been explored in the literature, but considerable work is required to understand these processes in the unequal playing field that shapes the experiences of those seeking and delivering care. In this book, I bring together critical perspectives for the study of health and disease to shed light on the infrastructures, empowerments, imaginaries, and affective relationships that play a role in international, regional, and local travel for medical services. I present examples from a wide range of studies on medical travel as well as my own ethnographic exploration of families' experiences of internal medical travel for cancer care in Argentina to demonstrate the value of using a critical (im)mobilities framework capable of recognizing the meanings and practices associated with different forms of movement and care.

CHAPTER TWO
Critical perspectives on medical travel

Social scientists working on healthcare related topics have drawn extensively from the work of critical theorists, mainly from the Frankfurt School, to examine societal inequalities, processes of domination as well as the ability of individuals to take part in collective action to subvert the social order (Waitzkin, 1991). The work of theorists such as Habermas has been used to highlight the ideologies engrained in science and medicine, which tend to legitimate and reproduce patterns of domination at class, gender, and ethnic levels, yet are obscured from the public due to the fact that both science and medicine are often presented as apolitical (Habermas, 1970). This ideological domination, which tends to favor the interests, needs, and ideas of some over others is also materialized in daily interactions and interpersonal relationships, maintaining hegemony and making it more difficult to question the status quo (Habermas, 1970; Waitzkin, 1991). These ideologies permeate the medical encounter, allowing certain configurations of care, and meanings associated with the role of the healthcare professional and the patient, whether care is obtained locally or far away from home (Waitzkin, 1991).

Elements from critical theory have been used to develop critical perspectives to explore processes of medical travel. In this chapter, I will present a brief overview of the main theoretical frameworks used to explore the use of travel to access care, which have been inspired by critical perspectives. I examine the work carried out in critical medical anthropology, critical medical geography, critical ethics, and post-colonial theory. I place emphasis on the critical (im)mobilities framework and present a series of ways in which it can be applied as the lens through which to visualize travel, care-seeking, and the delivery of medical services.

CRITICAL MEDICAL ANTHROPOLOGY (CMA)

Critical medical anthropology (CMA) recognizes that both health and care are shaped by class, gender, age, and ethnicity. Health and access to care are highly political, in the sense that they are dependent on market and government policies, decisions on the distribution of resources, cultural representations of populations who are 'deserving' and 'undeserving' of care, and the histories of healthcare systems (Singer & Baer, 2018). CMA recognizes the colonizing role of both anthropology and medicine; and seeks to change unequal and oppressive models of healthcare (Baer et al., 1986; Estroff, 1988; Pelto, 1988; Scheper-Hughes, 1990; Singer, 1989, 1990, 1995). Spatial and temporal arrangements of health and disease are analyzed in relation to power differentials both inside and outside medical spheres (Armstrong, 1988; Frankenberg, 1992). These power differentials influence individuals' timely access to medical institutions, their navigation of the health system, their adherence to treatment regimes, and the possibility of maintaining a healthy lifestyle. CMA acknowledges that health and care inequalities are in constant transformation and tries to understand the role of individual actors in the negotiation of barriers to care (Singer & Baer, 2018).

This anthropological framework allows us to view biomedicine as one of many explanatory models of health and disease, therefore acknowledging the value of other types of medicine (Singer, 1995). In doing so, it leads researchers to look at the different ways in which biomedical discourse became dominant throughout history and the role it has played in the constitution of modern societies, and the creation of specific subjects (Foucault, 1963; Waitzkin, 1991). CMA incorporates the anthropological, holistic approach and considers all aspects of human society when analyzing particular treatments or healthcare models (Singer, 1995).

This framework is based on the premise that medical knowledge and practice are neither homogeneous nor static and that "there exist institutional and situational openings for influence and activity at many points in health care systems" (Singer, 1995, p. 87). The recognition of historical backgrounds, contradictions in social relations, and imbalances of power in social categorizations (class, race, ethnicity, etc.) make CMA an adequate framework for understanding the factors that shape the treatment and movement experiences of patients at local and global levels.

CRITICAL MEDICAL GEOGRAPHY

The field of medical geography is diverse and centers on understanding the spatial relationships between health and care, and other factors that influence these (i.e. environment). While the term medical geography is widely used, it has been critiqued due to the limited spectrum of the term 'medical.' Other labels such as "post-medical geography of health" (Kearns, 1993) and, more recently, "geographies of health" (Gatrell & Elliott, 2009) have been proposed to encompass a wider range of care models. Initially, most studies implemented a positivistic analysis of space and the movement of individuals, relying mainly on quantitative methods and rigid forms of spatial measurement (Gatrell & Elliott, 2009, p. 24). Different attempts of theoretical transformation led to a conceptual expansion where social interactionist or constructionist perspectives privileging the concern over meaning, and the idea of place, came to play a more important role (Gatrell & Elliott, 2009). Originally proposed by Eyles (1985), place has been defined as "an interactive relationship between daily experience of a (local) place and perceptions of one's place-in-the-world" (Kearns & Gesler, 1998). When applied to the examination of patients' access to medical services, this idea of place becomes relevant in the sense that the hospital where care is provided is subjected to a constant attribution of personal meaning. These ideas and perceptions of place influence the patient's treatment experience and are intrinsically linked to families' decisions to migrate (Kangas, 2002). Previous negative experiences, rumors, and intuition conform what medical geographers have called emotional geographies, where people, places, and emotions intersect to create personal attitudes toward specific locales (Davidson et al., 2005; Milligan, 2007).

Particular destinations, sometimes referred to as landscapes, are sought because they are believed to provide relief and healing (denominated therapeutic landscapes) or avoided because they are associated with negative perceptions and feelings (landscapes of despair) (Gatrell & Elliott, 2009; Kearns & Collins, 2010). Landscapes have been defined as "the converging layers of history, social structure, and built environment at particular sites" (Kearns & Collins, 2010, p. 17). Therapeutic landscapes are those that "have achieved lasting reputations for providing physical, mental, and spiritual healing" (Kearns & Gesler, 1998, p. 8), including, for instance, spa towns, water springs, temples, gardens, etc. (Gesler, 1993, 1996). The concept of landscape includes the physical transformation of areas by human actions, the personal mental configuration of places, and the social and political construction of a specific region (Kearns & Gesler, 1998, pp. 7–8).

Critical perspectives have been incorporated in the field of medical geography to understand the uneven spatial development of health services and the impact of this unequal distribution on access to care, and, ultimately, the health of populations (Jenner, 2008). Individuals are able to negotiate these limitations demanding other forms of local care or bypassing local services and seeking care elsewhere (Ergler et al., 2011). However, some areas/populations are ultimately destined to receive fewer services or lower qualities of care than others (Warf, 2010), as global politics are reproduced in the delivery and access of medical services (Buzinde & Yarnal, 2012).

CRITICAL ETHICS

Medical travel processes have also been analyzed in the field of ethics, mainly through the concept of health as a universal human right and the exploration of equity in care (Smith, 2012). According to Pennings (2007), if access to healthcare is considered a universal human right, then access to services should be determined based on individual need and not on the capacity to pay for services. In practice, however, there is a constant interaction and tension between the representation of health as both a right and a commodity. These tensions are evident in the study of medical travel as health might be conceptualized as a commodity in some situations (i.e. when seeking cheaper services abroad), but not in others. The commodity/right tension is also present in the terminology used to describe processes of travel for medical services as discussed earlier in the book, where the term 'medical tourism' has been widely used, yet it is frequently considered problematic as it equates access to healthcare as optional and a luxury (Smith, 2012).

A critical ethics perspective highlights inequities in care, pointing to the ethical and moral dimensions of the distribution of services at a global level (Whitehead, 1991). Pennings (2015) has presented an in-depth discussion of the concept of distributive justice, arguing that different theories of justice can be used to evaluate the current medical travel system at a global scale. A theory of justice with a utilitarian view would seek to use resources in a way that well-being is maximized, while prioritarians would focus on those who require more assistance (Pennings, 2015). Egalitarians would seek equal care for all populations (at home and in destination areas) and sufficientarians would aim for care to be reasonably good (i.e. not falling below certain thresholds) (Pennings, 2007, 2015).

Debates on medical travel and equity of care could take on different characteristics depending on the theory of justice under consideration. When highlighting inequalities and access to care, are we assuming all individuals should have the same level of access or should some people be prioritized over others? When referring to the unequal distribution of services that forces some patients to travel to access care, are we considering these services as care that can be classified as good or bad based on pre-established standards or are we only considering high-quality care?

The critical ethics framework also raises questions around the moral issues and responsibilities associated with medical travel. Individuals in destination countries can be considered in a state of exploitation as their work, bodies, and body parts are used to heal foreign patients (Cohen, 2015). Medical travel can be seen as an appropriation and domination of local medical services by the medical travel industry, so critical ethicists raise the question of who has the moral obligation to address this domination. Should this be left to the destination areas or should medical travelers also play a role (Pennings, 2015; Smith, 2012; Turner, 2007)? Both Meghani (2011) and Snyder et al. (2013) have argued that medical travelers have a moral obligation to ensure the care they seek abroad is not delivered at the expense of the care of local populations and to seek ways to reduce harm. Yet, global assertions of the moral responsibility and potential harm of specific flows of traveling patients across the globe are still missing (Pennings, 2015).

POST-COLONIAL THEORY

A post-colonial perspective in medical geography views medical travel as a form of neocolonialism where structural relations of power maintain access to medical services for those in the core at the expense (and exploitation) of those in the peripheries (Buzinde & Yarnal, 2012). When using this lens, medical travel needs to consider the relationships between 'sending' and 'receiving' countries or regions and understand them in relation to a longstanding history of domination and resistance (Buzinde

& Yarnal, 2012; Ormond, 2013, 2015b). Medical travel can be seen as a new form of exploitation where countries who have dominated the geopolitical landscape take advantage of cheaper services, medical resources, and even body parts in 'dominated' areas of the globe (Buzinde & Yarnal, 2012).

Destinations participate in the medical travel industry by strategically selecting cultural features to lure medical travelers, a form of selective essentialism (Buzinde & Yarnal, 2012). This form of scripting and "rescripting" of multiculturalism discourse (Bunnell, 2002; Ormond, 2013) reproduces cultural representations of destination countries imposed during colonial rule, but it also contains negotiated and reformulated depictions of the country, its history, culture, and medical expertise (Buzinde & Yarnal, 2012). Within a heavily unequal medical travel system, destination countries are reworking what it means to deliver care to foreign patients based on the development of their own reputation as centers of excellence in subaltern locations. According to Ormond, this active reworking of cultural identity is the product of "the self-conscious development of a 'post-colonial political economy' based upon an alternative re-imagining of the 'global' that decenters the 'core' and multiplies the sites of which care knowledge and expertise are thought to flow" (2013, p. 93). By focusing on the case of Malaysia as one of the regional 'hot-spots' of medical travel, Ormond (2013) provides insight into the processes used by the Malaysian state to extend its territorial governance by gaining control of patient travel flows and national landmarks in cross-border areas.

CRITICAL (IM)MOBILITIES

The field of medical travel has grown considerably in the past decades, in relation to both empirical research and theoretical innovation. However, in many ways, medical travel research remains divorced from important conceptual and methodological work being carried out in other fields, such as mobility studies. This distance might limit our ability to think about and apply concepts relating to movement and stasis, both real and imagined. One of the aims of this book is to bring both of these fields together, and through existing research on medical travel, explore the potential contributions critical (im)mobilities can make to our understanding of experiences of medical travel, medical travel imaginaries, and the delivery of care to medical travelers. This chapter presents the framework that anchors the book, outlining the core concepts from critical (im)mobilities that could be productive in explorations of medical travel.

THE MOBILITIES PARADIGM

The social sciences have experienced a "mobilities turn," which critiqued fixed and sedentary notions of social life and drew our attention to the constant flows of people, ideas, and objects that permeate our daily lives (Urry, 2002). According to Soderström et al. (2013), the mobilities turn made three main contributions to the social sciences: (1) it argued that mobilities remained untheorized and should occupy central stage, (2) it proposed an ontological understanding of mobilities, where processes of movement were seen as (re)constituting the essence of things, people, and ideas in motion, (3) it demonstrated that a conceptual turn toward mobilities would also require methodological calibrations to capture flows, relationships, and multiple analytical scales.

By proposing to study mobilities "in their own singularity, centrality and contingent determination" (D'Andrea et al., 2011, p. 150), the mobilities paradigm created a new, dynamic, lens through which to (re)examine social thought and practice (Soderström et al., 2013, p. vi). This lens, according to Urry (2007), needed to be transformative, in the sense that the study of mobilities implied profound changes in our way to capture and understand social phenomena. These transformations would be produced by developing new metaphors based on movement (and not only on stasis), examining a wide range of mobility forms (corporeal, virtual, imagined), considering the complex relationships between people and objects, analyzing how class, gender, ethnicity, and nationhood cross-cut possibilities and experiences of travel and dwelling, and exploring changes in governmentality geared toward 'regulating' mobilities (Urry, 2007).

One of the aims of the mobilities paradigm was the exploration of the ways in which people, things, and ideas were formed and reshaped through movement. As Appadurai has argued, the meanings of objects "are inscribed in their forms, their uses, their trajectories" (1996, p. 5). Objects might maintain or lose their value while moving (Urry, 2007). The flows of objects and people also lead to the transformation of the spaces they traverse. In other words, the mobilities paradigm distanced itself from notions of spaces and objects as fixed, empty, and immutable (Hannam et al., 2006), and, instead, visualized objects, materials, and spaces as continuously in motion (Cresswell, 2011; Verstraete & Cresswell, 2002). As a consequence, additional attention was now paid to the ways in which objects, spaces, and infrastructures might allow or hinder movement (Hannam et al., 2006; Urry, 2007). Furthermore, the interactions between objects and people were understood in relation to affordances (a range of options within infinite possibilities based on capacities) that might incite some behaviors and inhibit others (Urry, 2002).

Another important contribution of the mobilities paradigm was the conceptualization of mobility forms as acting in dialectical relationship with the immobile, what Urry (2007) has called "moorings," where flows of people, information, or objects might be interrupted, fixed, or suspended at specific time points (Hannam et al., 2006; Salazar, 2016). Movement and stasis could not be understood separately, and research needed to understand the factors that both enabled and hindered movement (Adey, 2006). Recent work has highlighted the importance of thinking about a mobility/immobility continuum, where movement intersects with processes that might entail episodes of transition, waiting, emptiness, and fixity (Khan, 2016). The mobilities paradigm considers these spaces of limited or no movement as windows into the meanings, experiences, and practices of both moving or staying still.

A recognized limitation in mobilities research was the rigidity of research methods and their incapacity for capturing the richness and complexity of movement and stasis (Urry, 2007). An important component of the mobilities paradigm, then, needed to be the modification of existing methods or creation of new ones to capture diverse forms and modalities of (im)mobility (D'Andrea et al., 2011). Urry (2007) argued that methods needed to be "on the move," and proposed eight main ways for mobilizing methods: (1) observing mobile bodies, (2) participating in patterns of movement ("walking with" methods used in ethnographic research where researchers move with their participants), (3) recording movement through narratives (i.e. time-space diaries, where participants present records of their movement), (4) exploring virtual mobilities through social media and other forms of communication, (5) capturing the feelings of movement through oral and written expression (song, poetry, literature), (6) tracking objects and if and how these change through movement, (7) understanding "places of movement" and how these change, and (8) examining movement through "transfer points," places of transition or in-between-ness that individuals must inevitably go through.

Multi-sited ethnographies and mobile ethnographies have been used to document movement across both physical (i.e. fieldwork in multiple locales) and conceptual spaces (Marcus, 1995; Vergunst, 2011). Inhabiting the different spaces relevant to the topic under study gives the researcher insight into experiences of movement and how these spaces might shape objects, people, and ideas in motion (Vergunst, 2011). The emphasis is placed on the importance of 'being there' as an empirical approach.

Many innovative approaches for capturing movement relied on the use of tracking methods, shadowing or "walking along" techniques (Buscher & Urry, 2009; Laurier et al., 2008; Spinney, 2011). By participating in journeys with their participants, researchers obtained an approximation to their experience of movement, but were also able to capture the nuances of the structures that facilitated or hindered travel (Spinney, 2011). Researchers might "follow the thing" (Appadurai, 1996, p. 5), where they might physically move to follow things or people under study, but they might also capture movement through mapping or techniques of tracing that do not rely on movement (Salazar et al., 2017).

A recent volume has queried the need for mobile methods to capture movement, and, instead, highlights that, in some cases, being co-mobile might not be possible or desired (Salazar et al., 2017, p. 8). Mobility can be studied from acts of stillness, by remaining 'in place,' thus developing a perspective on movement that might be able to capture different aspects of flows and without relying on mobile approaches (Coates, 2017; Lindquist, 2009, p. 10).

The mobilities turn contributed to theoretical and methodological innovation in the social sciences, diversifying into different approaches for the study of (im)mobilities, such as Uteng and Cresswell's (2008) focus on gendered mobilities, Salazar's (2010b) proposal for cultural mobilities, and Jensen's (2013, 2014) exploration of the intersections between mobilities and art. Another approach, critical (im)mobilities, is interested in examining (im)mobilities as a way of gaining insight into patterns of asymmetrical power and privilege (Soderström et al., 2013, p. xi).

The integration of critical theory in mobility studies stems from the desire to unravel the social and political structures that shape our daily lives (Soderström et al., 2013). A focus on critical (im)mobilities attempts to move away from ideas of the world as given or taken for granted, and, instead, questions and critically analyzes the status quo (Adey & Bissell, 2010). It recognizes the profound historical roots of contemporary power regimes and the apparatuses used to maintain their hegemony (Cresswell, 2001). In this section, I propose three main dimensions for critical (im)mobilities: (1) the role of infrastructure in shaping different physical mobility trajectories, (2) the consideration of mobility as capital in creating differences in mobilities and imagined possibilities, and (3) experiential and affective mobilities.

INFRASTRUCTURES

The concept of infrastructure brings to light "the social structures and various material and institutional infrastructures" (Korpela, 2016) that create and recreate the frameworks within which movement is enacted. The analysis of infrastructures involved in mobilities engages with the materiality of movement and stasis; the objects, roads, networks, institutions that facilitate, constrain, or suspend movement (Urry, 2007). As Korpela has argued, "mobile subjects need infrastructures to realize their mobilities, but on the other hand, these infrastructures control and constrain people's mobilities" (2016, p. 114). In other words, infrastructures contribute to the creation of particular mobility subjectivities, as individuals have different capacities for mediating the infrastructure around them.

Power is, therefore, exercised and shaped through infrastructures, particularly by the state (Korpela, 2016). Lin et al. (2017) have encouraged us to look beyond the movement of particular groups, and, instead, visualize how *regimes* of travel are formulated to produce different types of journeys and migrancies. In doing so, we are able to capture the ways in which infrastructures might not only enable movement, but steer it in particular ways to create 'categories' of travelers (Lin et al., 2017, p. 168). Medical travel is made possible by a wide range of interacting structures which include national regulation of care, medical travel facilitators in the form of companies or brokers, and even virtual forms of infrastructure such as online patient communities.

Castañeda (2018) has worked with the concept of infrastructure when writing about undocumented migrants' experiences of accessing health services in the Texas/Mexico borderlands. She works with infrastructure produced by bordering processes that constrain the movement of undocumented migrants to the extent that they feel in a constant state of "stuckness." She refers to these migrants as being "stuck in motion" (Castañeda, 2018). This idea alludes to both fixity and motion, and is an attempt to consider the coexistence of mobility and immobility without succumbing to the restrictions of the dichotomy of movement/stasis (Khan, 2016). Mobilities and moorings intertwine to produce instances of stillness, fixity, and restraint (Hannam et al., 2006), but being stuck does not mean being immobile. The migrants Castañeda (2018) worked with shared the diverse strategies they use to negotiate borders, both lived and imagined, and restrictions in movement to obtain medical services, restore their health, and, in some cases, save the lives of their children. According to her, if we shift our conceptualization of borders from a fence or a wall to the stillness of people, we might be able to rethink borders as porous, dynamic, and inhabited places, places that change, have meaning, and matter (Castañeda, 2018).

Castañeda's (2018) work responds to more recent conceptualizations of the concept of infrastructures, where these are seen in a state of constant transformation from both a social and material point of view, "requiring physical maintenance, gathering meanings and generating atmospheres" (Merriman, 2016, p. 87). Infrastructures are reconfigured in daily practices that might create minor adaptations in their use, or the way in which they are conceived. According to Merriman (2016), instead of thinking about *infrastructures*, it might be more productive to think about *infrastructuring* to denote the changing nature of infrastructures, but also capture the ways in which these structures generate particular emotions, conceptions, experiences, and environments. The latter points to the performative dimensions of infrastructures. Harrison (2001) has argued that "things move through the world, or indeed move the world," highlighting not only the effect of infrastructures, but also the relational quality of infrastructures that conceptualizes these in a state of becoming (Cresswell, 2002). In this way, infrastructures can be seen as never complete, but always in a state of development.

In other words, infrastructures are not only the product of their material make-up, but are made and unmade by the relations between people, objects, and environments (Adey, 2006; Mackenzie, 2002; Thrift & French, 2002). Through an analysis of parking in the UK, Merriman (2016, p. 87) is able to show that spaces have "distinctive temporalities," where space might be interpreted and used differently depending on the time, person, or circumstance. In the case of medical travel, one of the infrastructures mentioned earlier, the hospital where the medical traveler receives care, is a good example of the temporalities of infrastructures. The building entered by the medical traveler might be the same physical building used by local patients, but as a place, that is, as a space charged with memories and emotions, it is a completely different environment. In many cases, the medical traveler is treated in a luxurious private room, with round-the-clock medical assistance, and an en-suite bathroom. The local patient might be only a few meters away in a bay, with shared bathroom and no night doctor cover. In the same way that mobility scholars have theorized about the airport as "an active and mobile participant" (Adey, 2006, p. 82), the hospital is not a fixed and stable infrastructure, it (re)configures itself based on the relations between people, time, and objects. It can never be complete, and is always in a state of becoming (Adey, 2006).

MOBILITY AS CAPITAL

A central component of the critical mobilities framework is the recognition that mobility is a process shaped by power relations. Not everyone who desires to move is able to do so and some people might be forced to move against their will (Skeggs, 2004; Morley, 2002). Mobility, then, is highly differentiated

(Adey 2006; Cresswell, 2001) and this differentiation is produced by the performance of movement in social worlds that are shaped by politics, history, economics, and cultures. As Tesfahuney has argued, "differential mobility empowerments reflect structures and hierarchies of power and position by race, gender, age and class, ranging from the local and the global" (1998, p. 501). These structures and hierarchies of power shape instances of mobility and immobility (Urry, 2003), and the mobility of some can even weaken or eliminate the capacity to move of others (Massey, 1991, p. 240).

Movement and stasis are highly contextual, but what might be at the core of differential mobility empowerments is the capacity to move when movement is desired, the ability to have freedom of movement (Sager, 2006). As Adey has argued, "mobility is attributed with an emancipatory power" (2006, p. 77), as it can be the means through which to transgress material and symbolic power structures as well as engender and sustain social relations with individuals who are not necessarily close or proximate (Larsen & Urry, 2008, p. 93). These relations with those who are not proximate play a central role in mobility due to our reliance on co-presence (Bærenholdt, 2013), that is, "moments of physical proximity to particular peoples, places or events" (Urry, 2002, p. 258). The capacity to travel to have these face-to-face encounters is a powerful determinant of the social relations we are able to create and sustain (Bærenholdt, 2013). In other words, it is the need for co-presence that generates mobility (Simmel, 1997).

Co-presence represents a useful concept when thinking about medical travel, as the need to be in close proximity to medical professionals is the reason why most patients will physically travel to other locations. However, not everyone will have the capacity to perform this movement, making co-presence a luxury only available for some. As evident in the work of Speier in reproductive medical travel, only those US couples able to travel to the Czech Republic for donor eggs would have the opportunity to conceive a child (Speier, 2016). An interesting aspect of the application of the concept of co-presence to medical practice is the fact that the need for co-presence in care delivery is changing. This change has been mainly produced by technological advances that facilitate remote monitoring of patient conditions and online communication between doctors and patients. In the case of medical travel, patients might now be receiving some care locally before (i.e. diagnostic tests) and after returning home from a procedure (i.e. follow-up care). Some healthcare systems might also seek to limit the times patients need to travel by engaging in virtual forms of care such as telemedicine (Brage, 2018).

It will be important to consider gradients of co-presence across the pathway of care and the role mobility plays in ensuring proximity is accomplished when it is required, but how can we account for the fact that some people are able to achieve this proximity while others cannot? Some authors have argued that mobility can be considered a resource and tend to use the concept of mobility capital to explain the degree to which individuals are able to negotiate their mobility and restrictions imposed on their movement (Kaufmann, 2002; Kaufmann et al., 2004; Jensen, 2011). This concept alludes to factors that act as preconditions for mobility, affordances, or predispositions that facilitate movement (Murphy-Lejeune, 2002).

Other authors have taken this concept even further, proposing the idea of capital, referred to, in this case, as network capital, to explore the ability to move as well as to stay still. As Urry (2002) has argued, "it's sometimes those with more network capital who are the immobile, who can summon the mobile to where they are." The concept of network capital considers competences of movement, connections with people, transportation options, access to information, communication channels, and legal regulation (Jayaram, 2016). Network capital is interlaced with other forms of capital (i.e. social, cultural, and economic capital) to enable some forms of travel and hinder others, reproducing inequalities in both movement and stasis. Consideration of different forms of mobility capital (Kaufmann, 2002) or differential mobility empowerments (Tesfahuney, 1998) is another useful layer of analysis of the power relations and inequalities in the context of medical travel.

IMAGINED MOBILITIES AND POSSIBILITIES

An important contribution of the work of mobility scholars has been the emphasis placed on the role played by the imagination in determining the potential for mobility and shaping experiences of movement (Lean et al., 2014). Salazar conceptualizes imaginaries as "socially transmitted representational assemblages that interact with people's personal imaginings and are used as meaning-making and world-shaping devices" (2012, p. 864). Imagination can act as a trigger for traveling as it creates, in the anticipation of a future encounter, the desire for proximity or near-ness of others (Habeck & Broz, 2015). Experienced journeys can diverge from how they were originally imagined. Vivid imagined journeys can also remain in the imaginary and never materialize (Salazar, 2013). These journeys that will never happen, however, still play an important role in the development of subjectivities as they inform configurations of the self, local places, and imagined destinations (Conradson & McKay, 2007).

This potential mobility, or mobility that is never enacted or remains incomplete (Leivestad, 2016), has been referred to as motility (Kaufmann, 2002; Kaufmann et al., 2004). Leivestad argues that this incompleteness transforms motility as the lens through which we can examine aspiration for movement as mobility appears "yet-to-be realized, yet-to-be-completed or never-to-be" (2016, p. 134). These aspirations are not (re)configured in a vacuum, they are the product of social, cultural, and political contexts (Appadurai, 2003). In many ways, we learn how to imagine and how to aspire; our understanding of possibilities is socially constructed. As a result, motility is also unevenly and unequally distributed, as the potential for mobility is not available to all. In the case of medical travel, not everyone who needs life-saving treatment is able to imagine seeking it elsewhere.

AFFECTIVE (IM)MOBILITIES

A critical mobilities framework should also consider more symbolic dimensions of mobility and stasis. Some of these dimensions were explored in the previous section on imagination, but in addition to imagination, attention should be paid to complex webs of feelings or emotions that are stimulated through the act of movement, thinking about movement, or remaining still (Sheller & Urry, 2006). Considerable work has been carried out in anthropology and geography to highlight the emotions associated with places, the act of moving and how individuals might experience multiple forms of ongoing emplacement (as in the case of migrants who continue to experience strong connections to their place of origin) (Boellstorff & Lindquist, 2004; Conradson & McKay, 2007; Davidson et al., 2005).

The concept of affect has been used frequently to explore "embodied states" that are constructed through particular mixtures or assemblages (Thrift, 2004). For Spinoza (2001), emotions are seen as the mechanism of expression of our bodies (see also Deleuze & Guattari, 1994). Emotions are seen as the perception and expression of affects through cultural mediation and language (Conradson & McKay, 2007), thus, leading to local variation that can be explored cross-culturally. The desire to experience particular emotions might be a trigger for movement, for instance, the desire to feel happiness or a sense of security through proximity with friends or relatives. Embodied states accompany movement, making those who travel experience their own sense of selfhood, purpose, and belonging (Lean et al., 2014).

Destinations, places of origin, places in-between, and modes of transport will all create particular environments that stimulate the senses and create unique emotional states. Harvey and Knox (2012), for instance, argue that infrastructures, in the form of roads, have the capacity to generate a sense of enchantment, that is, a potential surprising encounter or unexpected event. Roads create a sense of promise, of "illusory plausibility" (Harvey & Knox, 2012, p. 254), that can be used for different purposes, including political promises for development, speed, economic connectivity, and social integration (Harvey & Knox, 2012).

In this sense, emotional and affective states should also be considered within the material dimensions explored earlier in the chapter, as emotions are shaped by processes of unequal power relations. Salazar's (2011) ethnographic study of tourism discourses and practices among village guides on the island of Java illustrates this point. Village guides experienced tension between imagining themselves as cosmopolitan world travelers and being represented by tourists as local. Their dreams of mobility and imagined possibilities of a better life were sometimes shattered, creating negative emotions, as they encountered the harsh realities of not being able to move. According to Salazar, "the opening of wider horizons and the multiplication imagined and fascinating life possibilities also makes exclusion and frustration increasingly evident" (2011, p. 594). In an analysis of Deleuzian perspectives in research, Ringrose and Coleman argue that an important aspect of our study of affect and emotions lies in considering political dimensions of subjectivities by asking "what can bodies do and not do?" (Ringrose & Coleman, 2013, p. 127).

The possibility of seeking care elsewhere is capable of generating new emotions. As Kangas (2007) has argued, global connectivity can change perceptions of the care available to patients, as they no longer need to restrict themselves to what is available locally. In a way, the possibility to travel to seek care elsewhere enacts feelings of hope as the chance of finding relief or a cure are now plausible. Emotional states prevalent during travel (i.e. wonder, anxiety, fear, excitement) are compounded by emotions associated with diagnosis (i.e. uncertainty) and treatment (i.e. hope), creating a complex web of feelings for those seeking and delivering care. Emotions guide decisions to seek care elsewhere, they influence the selection of destinations, shape the experience of care and permeate stories of medical travel told to others upon return. Emotions also guide the carework performed by professionals delivering services to patients as well as those who travel with patients who seek care elsewhere.

Emotions of and during medical travel also need to be understood in relation to socio-political and economic contexts where frustration, exclusion, and embarrassment might be experienced by certain patient groups. For instance, in my research on Bolivian and Paraguayan parents seeking care for their ill children in Argentina, a prevalent issue in their stories of medical travel were experiences of discrimination. Many of the parents who shared their experiences with me described instances where they felt underserving of medical care and were portrayed as 'draining' the Argentine public health system of its scarce resources. These feelings had a direct impact on their lived experience, identity, and perceptions of Argentine society. They felt trapped in a system that represented them as underserving of care because of their place of origin.

CONCLUSIONS

In this chapter, I have presented the critical (im)mobilities framework as the lens through which we can explore experiences of medical travel. Following the mobilities turn in the social sciences, this framework considers (im)mobilities as its main subject of study, not as an expression of other phenomena. A particular characteristic of the framework is its emphasis on the role of hierarchies and asymmetrical power relations on arrangements of mobility and immobility, and, in this book, I explore the impact of these asymmetries on access and delivery of medical care. I have teased out three main concepts from critical (im)mobilities that I believe are helpful for exploring medical travel.

A focus on infrastructures, as structures enabling and hindering travel, sheds light on the complex webs of actors involved in medical travel, both visible and hidden. Through terms such as infrastructuring, it also highlights the changing nature and continuous negotiation of these structures and how these might vary depending on the actors involved. The critical (im)mobilities framework also considers the use of (im)mobility as capital, that is, as a potential resource to gain proximity, escape or stay still, if these are desired. This capital interacts with other forms of capital (economic, social, symbolic) to create certain predispositions or affordances of movement for some and not for others. In the case of medical travel, this can very well mean the difference between life and death, if patients need to travel due to life-threatening conditions.

The critical (im)mobilities framework also underscores the importance of the imagination and emotions on decisions to travel and the experience of travel itself. Imagined journeys are shaped by our social context as there are only some journeys we might conceive possible. Our feelings become intertwined with these imagined possibilities to guide decisions on which journeys to undertake and how (seeking adventure, eliciting hope) or to exhibit a sense of frustration and anger if these journeys cannot be enacted.

In sum, the critical (im)mobilities framework allows us to critically examine the material, performative, imaginative, and affective inequalities in medical travel across the globe. This multidimensional lens can make important contributions to future studies of medical travel. In the next chapter, I will discuss the current global state of medical travel, as well as the research carried out on this topic to date.

CHAPTER THREE
Medical travel at a global scale

Medical travel is a complex phenomenon that has undergone various transformations over time. The flows of patients have diversified to include travel from the Global South to the North, or vice versa, and from the North to the North as well as South to South travel. The reasons why patients decide to travel also vary (economic factors, availability, to reduce waiting time, to obtain culturally appropriate care) and many times patients express multiple reasons why they have decided to obtain care away from their place of origin. There are key assumptions underlying the promotion of the medical travel industry, many of which are not experienced in practice. Although the industry has developed considerably in recent decades, there are challenges around regulation, equity, management of complications and compensation in cases of malpractice that still remain. In this chapter, I will provide a review of the current state of medical travel at a global scale and the ways in which academic research has grappled with some of the main issues concerning travel and the delivery of care. I also outline some gaps and areas for future research.

THE SCALE OF MEDICAL TRAVEL

Bookman and Bookman (2007) have indicated that processes of globalization have created transformations in the ways in which medical attention is sought abroad. According to them, the reduction in transportation costs, the increase in quantity and access to information, and the liberalization of health services and trade have contributed to the explosion of medical travel (Bookman & Bookman, 2007, p. 4). These factors have not only increased the volume of patients traveling to other countries, but also the frequency of travel and the variety of treatments sought abroad. I would also argue that the processes set out by Bookman and Bookman (2007) have contributed to the development of intra-regional medical travel (travel within defined regions such as US patients crossing the border to Mexico, Western Europeans traveling to East European countries, hospitals in Thailand delivering care to patients from neighboring countries such as Vietnam, Burma, and Cambodia; see Cohen, 2010; Lunt et al., 2014), and even intra-national medical travel (travel within countries).

In the case of international medical travel, the number of patients seeking care abroad allows us to see the scale of this growing industry. For instance, a report published more than ten years ago estimated that almost 1.6 million US patients sought medical services in another country (Keckley & Underwood, 2008), and, around the same time, Thailand reported delivering care to over one million patients from the US and Europe per year (Department of Export Promotion, Ministry of Commerce, in Pachanee, 2009). In terms of intra-regional travel, Toyota and colleagues (2013) have reported that almost 90% of foreign patients treated in Malaysia are from Indonesia, and Malaysian and Indonesian patients travel frequently to Singapore for care (cited in Chee, 2010). In 2010, an annual growth of the medical travel industry was expected at a rate of 20% (Helbe, 2011).

Intra-national medical travel is more difficult to estimate as hospitals might not distinguish between local patients and those traveling from other areas of the country. Some countries, such as Argentina, have established disease-specific and patient group-specific registries that capture (and seek to highlight) the internal mobility of patients. The ROHA is a national registry of pediatric oncology patients and it records the place of origin of patients and their place of treatment. ROHA reports present a detailed analysis of numbers of patients seeking care outside of their place or residence, a process referred to as "assistance migration" (ROHA, 2008). In 2015, it was estimated that over 40% of children with cancer in Argentina received care outside of their place of residence (ROHA, 2018).

MEDICAL TRAVEL FLOWS

People have always traveled to improve their health and obtain medical services. The first notable flows of traveling patients originated in the Global South and made their way to centers of excellence in the Global North (Cormany & Baloglu, 2011; Ormond, 2015b). Clinics in the US such as the Mayo Clinic or Johns Hopkins Hospital were often visited to obtain highly specialized or experimental treatment that was not available anywhere else (Johnston et al., 2012; Ormond, 2013).

The flows of medical travel then gradually diversified to also include journeys of patients in the Global North who sought medical care in facilities in the Global South in order to find cheaper services, quicker services, services not available in their home country, or seek care in a more private or confidential environment. An example of these flows that is normally used is that of North Americans seeking care in countries such as India, Thailand, or Malaysia. A liver transplant costing $300,000 in the US could be performed for $90,000 in India (Perfetto & Dholakia, 2010, p. 401), and a cardiac procedure, which might cost $60,000 in the US could cost around $12,000 in Thailand and as little as $3000 in India (Hazarika, 2010).

If we only considered these flows, we would be leaving out a significant portion of medical travel activity. An important set of flows are those of patients who seek care outside of their countries, but remain in the geographic region (Ormond, 2013). An example of this type of intra-regional travel includes the Association of South-East Asian Nations (ASEAN), where member countries have established a framework for trade collaboration and region-wide integration in relation to the delivery of healthcare (Arunanondcha & Fink, 2007). Countries such as Thailand received 630,000 patients from other countries in this region in 2002 (Arunanondcha & Fink, 2007) and Malaysia received 360,000 patients in 2007 (Helbe, 2011).

Cross-border care has been identified as one form of intra-regional medical travel. This involves patients who will visit neighboring countries for services through pre-established arrangements between countries or as a result of arrangements made by the patient. Some researchers have explored the experiences of North American patients who travel to Mexico for dental care (Cohen, 2010). India has reported receiving nearly 50,000 patients from Bangladesh every year (Helble, 2011). I have also analyzed the experiences of parents from Bolivia and Paraguay who traveled to Argentina to obtain pediatric oncology treatment for their ill children (Vindrola-Padros & Whiteford, 2012).

Medical travel flows are not only defined by geographic scale, but also vary in relation to other features of the patient, the services required and the care that is available. Connell (2013a) has argued that we should combine notions of intent, procedure, and duration to properly understand the wide range of patient categories seeking care outside of their place of origin. He distinguishes between elite patients seeking care for exclusive and costly treatment, middle-class patients seeking elective treatment like cosmetic surgery, patients referred by their own national governments, diasporic patients of diverse economic status returning to their home countries to access care, cross-border patients (some clandestine and others part of bilateral agreements), and 'desperate' medical travelers who travel despite the financial burden to access life-sparing treatment (Connell, 2013a).

The financing of travel might also generate particular medical travel flows as some patients might be paying for procedures out of pocket, while others might be sent abroad by their own governments with all expenses paid. Helbe (2011) has argued that medical travel has been used by uninsured or under-insured US patients who would never be able to afford care locally. Some health insurance companies now include medical treatment abroad as part of some of their cover packages (Helbe, 2011). Four US insurance companies provide reimbursement for procedures obtained in Thailand, India, and Mexico (Pocock & Phua, 2011). Some public healthcare systems, as in the case of Canada or the UK, routinely send patients abroad for procedures because waiting times are long due to limited capacity (Crooks et al., 2013). This might have negative local consequences as countries might be reluctant to address capacity issues locally, as patient cases can be dealt with elsewhere (Helbe, 2011).

An additional dimension of medical travel flows, one that requires additional attention in the literature, is that of intra-national flows. For some authors, this type of flow should not be referred to as medical travel, as they define medical travel as "travel beyond national jurisdiction for healthcare treatment, with the primary aim of obtaining that treatment" (Lunt et al., 2014). However, as this book attempts to demonstrate, travel within a country to access care shares many of the same mobility characteristics and challenges as international travel and deserves equal scholarly attention. As argued above, an important issue when attempting to study intra-national medical travel is the fact that patient flows are not always recorded, complicating the estimation of the increase or decrease in the number of patients seeking care away from their place of origin, but within national boundaries. An analysis of intra-national medical travel would expand our understanding of medical travel flows, considering the nuances of local displacement.

REASONS FOR TRAVEL

Most of the early literature on medical travel explained patients' reasons for travel to another location to access care in relation to economic factors (Connell, 2006). Patients would be faced with expensive procedures in their place of origin and would search the market for cheaper options (Connell, 2006). This led to the representation of the patient as an avid consumer who would choose to pay $7500 for a coronary bypass in Thailand vs. $100,000 in the US (Perfetto & Dholakia, 2010). Although economic factors exert some level of influence over patients' decision to travel and their travel destination, empirical research on patients' decision-making processes has indicated that there are a wide range of reasons why patients decide to engage in medical travel and interact to produce highly complex decision-making processes (Johnston et al., 2012).

In addition to treatment costs, many patients seek treatment abroad to reduce waiting times for procedures (Connell, 2006). This is particularly the case in countries with strong public healthcare systems (e.g. Canada, UK), which might be overwhelmed by patient demand and suffering from constraints such as staff shortages and other types of limited capacity (Johnston et al., 2012). Connell (2006) notes that waiting times for non-essential surgery such as knee reconstruction in the UK can take up to 18 months, while in India the procedure and recovery would be done in up to 17 days. Waiting time for fertility treatment can also be long in countries such as the UK (Connell, 2006).

Availability of treatment or procedures also plays a role in decisions to engage in medical travel. Availability takes on different connotations and it can mean: (1) the procedure/treatment is not available at all in the home country/region, (2) the procedure/treatment is not legal in the home country/region (Connell, 2006), or (3) the patient has not been able to get a referral or is not able to access the procedure/treatment in the home country/region (for instance, is ineligible due to age or other reasons) (Johnston et al., 2012). The literature on treatments/procedures not available at all in the patient's place of origin has mainly explored the journeys of patients traveling abroad to access experimental therapies such as stem cell therapies (Cohen, 2015; Song, 2010). The search for treatments that are not legal in the patient's place of origin has mainly focused on cases of euthanasia (Cohen, 2015; Connell, 2006, 2013a; Higginbotham, 2011) or some assisted reproductive technologies such as in-vitro fertilization with ova donation, which are illegal in countries such as Germany (Bergmann, 2011a, 2011b).

Some patients, however, might also need to travel to access procedures they were not personally able to obtain in their area of residence. In their study of Canadian patients' decisions to engage in medical travel, Johnston and colleagues (2012) found that some patients who were denied surgical procedures in Canada because their conditions were deemed inoperable by their domestic physician, sought the same procedure abroad. Another example has been the restricted number of in-vitro fertilization attempts covered by national health insurance and the travel endured by patients requiring additional cycles (Runnels & Carrera, 2012).

Some patients might also seek treatment abroad as these facilities might provide services while guaranteeing anonymity (Connell, 2006). This need for privacy has been documented in the case of gender reassignment surgery as patients decide to seek these treatments in countries like Thailand, where it might be easier to establish a new identity (Aizura, 2010; Connell, 2006). The search for 'discretion' for procedures such as cosmetic surgery or hair restoration has also been documented (Andrews, 2004; Connell, 2006).

Patients might also be traveling to access more culturally appropriate care or might choose to combine biomedical treatment with other forms of care. In India, for instance, medical travelers are able to access a wide range of allopathic and alternative systems of medicine (Hazarika, 2010). Hazarika (2010) explains how, while New Delhi has emerged as a core destination for cardiac care, Kerala and Karnataka are currently seen as centers for Ayurvedic healing.

Patients might also travel back to their countries of origin, a process referred to as return medical travel or tourism, to seek care in an environment they are more comfortable with. Inhorn (2011) has written about 'diasporic dreaming' in the case of Middle Eastern couples who imagine and plan accessing assisted reproductive technologies back home. Lee and colleagues (2010) have explored the relationship between health and place in their study of the journeys of Koreans residing in New Zealand, who travel back to their home country to access surgical services.

ASSUMPTIONS AND 'MYTHS' OF MEDICAL TRAVEL

Some of the literature on medical travel has pointed to 'master narratives' of medical travel (Cohen, 2010) or underlying assumptions that guide the discourse on the desires of patients seeking care away from home, sites delivering care to foreign patients and the relationship between these and the (re)production of this global industry. When examined in detail, the evidence to support these assumptions is limited and most of them do not take place in practice. In this section, I will explore these assumptions, synthesizing how they have been explored in the literature and the evidence that has been used to question them.

One of the guiding assumptions of medical travel is the inevitable development of this industry as a result of globalization, where health is not seen as a public good, but as a commodity that can be managed through international trade agreements (Cohen, 2010; Ormond, 2011, 2013). The representation of medical travel as a component of economic globalization has tended to reproduce early representations of globalization as a global process leading to the creation of a 'flat world,' where everyone would have access to the same information, services, capacity to travel, etc. As such, every person has the potential to become a future consumer, giving the medical travel market the potential for limitless long-term exponential growth (Lunt et al., 2014).

If health is seen as a good that can be traded, then it will generate profit and one dominant assumption is the belief that medical travel (particularly in the case of foreign patients from affluent countries) will lead to local economic growth, as the revenue from this service trade will spill into other areas of the economy or public sector (Garcia-Altes, 2005; Lunt et al., 2014; Ormond, 2013; Ramirez de Arellano, 2007; Smith, 2012). Some of this income (and potential income generated through taxation) would be used to improve existing healthcare facilities and the training of local healthcare staff, thus benefiting the local population seeking care in these facilities (Helbe, 2011; Ramirez de Arellano, 2007; Smith, 2012). Other parts of the income could be used to improve non-healthcare related facilities such as hotels and transport, or invested in public services, such as the education system (Helbe, 2011). The development of the national healthcare system would help to reduce the brain drain of healthcare workers as these would be more willing to stay in the country due to more financial incentives and better opportunities for career development (Pocock & Phua, 2011).

The medical traveler often epitomizes the independent, discerning and avid consumer who is empowered to review all available care options and make an informed and rational decision to travel for treatment (Runnels & Carrera, 2012). This assumption follows a neoliberal logic where patient choice emerges as a result of true emancipation from the market for medical travelers and their independent role as consumers (Ormond, 2011; Perfetto & Dholakia, 2010). Ormond (2013) has proposed the term 'patient-consumer' to account for the ways in which medical travelers are often perceived as patients who 'escape' their home health systems and negotiate good deals for health services purchased abroad. This concept of the medical traveler assumes that the main reason why patients travel for care is due to economic factors, where they seek to get the best value for money (Cohen, 2010).

Needless to say, when these assumptions have been tested in practice, they have not been found with the same intensity as described above or are missing completely in the evidence generated by empirical research. A substantial amount of theoretical and empirical work has demonstrated that the 'flat world' representation is a 'myth' as globalization is shaped by longstanding economic, political, social, and cultural processes, reproducing power relations and inequalities in access to resources (Appadurai, 1996). The arguments made by medical travel promoters mirror those presented by globalization theorists who believe that globalization "entails a shift from two-dimensional Euclidian space with its centers and peripheries and sharp boundaries, to a multidimensional global space with unbounded, often discontinuous and interpenetrating sub-spaces" (Kearney, 1995, p. 549). A trend has been to represent these processes of deterritorialization as having the potential to liberate individuals, communities, identities, or economic processes from clearly bounded and delimited spaces.

One of the main limitations of seeing the increase in global flows of people, goods, and ideas as liberating and homogenizing is that not enough attention is paid to the politics of time and space. Harvey (1989) has proposed that contemporary capitalist political economy is based on a form of time-space compression where relocation and faster production benefits companies while reducing the labor protection and opportunities of laborers. Furthermore, regional economic differentiation is exacerbated and access to employment is reduced for specific populations (Kearney, 1995). The increase in mobility needs to be understood within previously established regimes of power where territorial limitations still have tangible consequences on the lives of individuals (Ong, 1999).

In the case of medical travel, healthcare close to home as well as in the destination area is heavily influenced by historical, political, cultural, and economic factors. Meghan Ormond has carried out a significant amount of work on understanding medical travel from the point of view of destination countries and has argued that medical travel cannot be viewed as an external process 'invading' local economies (Ormond, 2011, 2013, 2015b). According to her, medical travel needs to be considered within local processes shaping healthcare delivery, such as the history of the privatization of healthcare, where the representation of health and care have shifted from health as a universal right to health as a commodity (Ormond, 2013). Medical travel is incorporated and reworked into existing logics and structures that have promoted the perception and implementation of health and care as commodities.

Another critique that has been made in relation to the 'flat world' idea is that not all medical travel journeys are the same. Not all patients will have access to the same information, services, or ability to travel. They also travel for a wide range of reasons as established above, and each motivation for travel shapes the journey and experience of care in particular ways. Each medical travel destination has appropriated the principles of medical travel in slightly different ways, infusing them with their own local smells and flavors. Buzinde and Yarnal (2012), for instance, have highlighted how destination countries often adopt strategic essentialism to reproduce stereotypes of exotic locations to lure medical travelers and compete with other destination countries. Ormond (2013) has focused on what she calls the 'cultural hybridity' of destination countries, where patients are attracted to locations that can deliver high-quality care, but also fulfill specific cultural requirements (e.g. delivering 'Muslim-friendly' care in Malaysia).

The limitless growth potential of this industry has also been criticized, and existing figures on the numbers of patients seeking care away from home have been queried. In their exploration of the myths of medical travel, Lunt and colleagues (2014) have argued that most of the commonly used figures of medical travel activity, revenue, and growth come from the medical travel industry itself, raising validity concerns. After analyzing projections made over ten years ago on the growth of the medical travel industry, these authors found that the projected numbers of medical travelers have not been met (Lunt et al., 2014). They have also pointed to problems with the raw data and methods used to make the calculation of projections of the growth of the industry (Lunt et al., 2014).

Authors have also warned that the relationship between the development of the medical travel industry in destination countries and 'spillover' of the revenue into other areas of the economy and public services is not simple or linear (Chen & Flood, 2013). Adequate taxation systems are required to collect the income, but countries also require clear mechanisms for redistributing the funds to other areas and these are often missing (Helbe, 2011; Chen & Flood, 2013). Furthermore, facilities delivering care to medical travelers are often private and will have a certain degree of autonomy on how they decide to spend or invest the funds obtained from medical travel (Chen & Flood, 2013).

The assumption that medical travel will raise the standards of care and improve access to more advanced technologies for the local population is even more difficult to prove as the evidence has pointed to the opposite picture (Connell, 2006, 2013a; Hopkins et al., 2010; Smith et al., 2011). Research from India, Malaysia, and Thailand has indicated that the local population is often faced with an increase in the cost of medical services, fewer care options (as these facilities become reserved for foreign private patients) and a decrease in the access to services and healthcare professionals (as many healthcare workers choose to work in private facilities delivering care to medical travelers due to the attractive salaries, facilities, and opportunities for career development) (Chen & Flood, 2013; Hazarika, 2010; Kassim, 2009). Several authors have highlighted the existence of two-tiered or multiple-tiered healthcare systems where higher standards of care and better facilities are available for medical travelers and lower standards characterize the care delivered to the local population (Pocock & Phua, 2011; Smith, 2012).

The ultimate consequence of the promotion of medical travel in many countries has been the creation of multiple-tiered healthcare systems with the lowest tier for the poorest local social classes, a middle tier for local middle and upper classes, and the highest tier for foreign private patients (Pocock & Phua, 2011). Additional work might need to be carried out to unpack these tiers even more and identify any potential hierarchies between medical travelers. Are intra-regional medical travelers considered in a different tier than international medical travelers coming from countries that are farther away (i.e. US or European countries)?

Authors have also queried the validity of the concept of the independent medical traveler who is emancipated from local and market constraints (Ormond, 2013; Perfetto & Dholakia, 2010; Smith, 2012). In their analysis of consumer agency and market emancipation in the case of medical travel, Perfetto and Dholakia (2010) found that despite finding a potential escape from constraints in access to services, US 'patient-consumers' continue to find themselves immersed in a medical travel market with its own social, political, and economic constraints, and a new set of rules and regulations they must learn and navigate. The market, then, reproduces inequalities in access to care.

CHALLENGES AND POTENTIAL RISKS OF MEDICAL TRAVEL

An in-depth analysis of the assumptions outlined above points to the prevalence of challenges or issues of concern in relation to medical travel that remain until today. A central challenge is the regulation of healthcare facilities providing care to medical travel patients, medical travel facilitation agencies, and other forms of intermediaries (Cohen, 2010; Connell, 2013a; Hazarika, 2010; Kassim, 2009; Penney et al., 2011; Pocock & Phua, 2011; Smith et al., 2011). One way in which regulation has been approached is through the accreditation of medical facilities abroad (Turner, 2011). According to Connell (2010), this is the main way in which foreign medical establishments can convince potential medical travelers of the quality and reliability of the services they provide (see also Warf, 2010). Prestigious international accreditation agencies such as the Joint Commission International (JCI), Accreditation Canada, the Australian Council for Healthcare Standards and the Society for International Healthcare Accreditation provide credibility to some medical facilities, but the proliferation of small-scale local accrediting organizations has casted doubt over accreditation processes in general (Connell, 2010, 2013a; Crooks et al., 2013; Smith et al., 2011). In 2012, 370 international hospitals had been accredited by the JCI (Runnels & Carrera, 2012). Two-thirds of JCI-accredited hospitals are in Asia, while one-fifth can be found in Europe (Runnels & Carrera, 2012).

An important issue with accreditation is the fact that it has tended to focus on private medical facilities, limiting the opportunities afforded to public hospitals to participate in the delivery of care to foreign patients. In the case of India, Hazarika (2010) argued that the JCI had accredited 13 facilities and all were in the private sector. This contributed to a decrease in the utilization of public medical facilities even by the local population, leading to the widening of the gap between the private and public sectors (Hazarika, 2010).

In their review of risk communication and informed consent in the medical travel industry, Penney and colleagues (2011) have expressed concern in relation to the incomplete or misleading information about the risks of medical travel provided by medical travel broker websites. According to the authors, this issue might limit patients' abilities to make informed decisions, posing a grave ethical concern (Penney et al., 2011; see also Crooks et al., 2013). Cormany and Baloglu (2011) identified a similar trend and found that the type of information included in medical travel websites varied by continent. This variability in information draws our attention to the need for global external regulation of actors acting as facilitators or brokers in medical travel (Cormany & Baloglu, 2011; Penney et al., 2011). European websites need to adhere to the European Union e-commerce directive (2000/31/EC), which requires all websites to include contact information (name of provider, geographic address, email, and telephone number or contact form) (Lunt et al., 2010). The extent to which similar regulations could be enforced at a global scale remains to be seen.

An important challenge in medical travel is the promotion of this industry without jeopardizing the care delivered to local populations. A significant number of studies have highlighted the negative impact of medical travel on destination healthcare systems (Chen & Flood, 2013; Hazarika, 2010; Kassim, 2009; Pachanee & Wibulpolprasert, 2006; Pocock & Phua, 2011). The main negative consequences that have been identified to date include: (1) the escalation of costs of treatment for local populations (Chen & Flood, 2013; Connell, 2006; Hazarika, 2010; Kassim, 2009), (2) brain drain of healthcare workers from rural to urban areas and from the public to the private healthcare sectors (Chen & Flood, 2013; Connell, 2013a; Hazarika, 2010; Hopkins et al., 2010; Smith et al., 2011), (3) lack of access of local patients to specialized procedures or technologies as these are reserved for foreign private patients (Chen & Flood, 2013), (4) lower quality of care delivered to local populations at public healthcare facilities (Smith et al., 2011), and (5) a shift in government priorities from public health and primary care to tertiary care (Bookman & Bookman, 2007; Connell, 2013a; Ramirez de Arellano, 2007). Cost of medical services is often increased for the local population. In the case of India, where patients are responsible for 80% of healthcare expenses, the increase in medical travel demand led to an increase in overall healthcare costs of between 55 and 77% over a 10-year period in the rural sector and between 76 and 116% in the urban sector (Hazarika, 2010).

Internal brain drain has been documented in some of the 'hot-spots' of medical travel (Wibulpolprasert & Pengpaibon, 2003). Increase in patient demand, financial incentives, and lower workloads in the private sector lead healthcare workers to migrate from medical facilities in rural areas to urban ones or from the public to the private sector (Pocock & Phua, 2011; Wibulpolprasert & Pachanee, 2008). In the case of Thailand, doctors experienced the greatest income gap between the private and public sectors, explaining why this is the professional group with the highest level of outflow in the country (Pannarunothai et al., 1998). Almost 6000 positions for physicians in public hospitals remained unfilled in Thailand in 2005 (Hopkins et al., 2010) and only 25–30% of specialists worked in the public sector in Malaysia (Pocock & Phua, 2011). Internal brain drain also poses questions in relation to the public funding used to train medical professionals who will then leave to work in the private sector (Pocock & Phua, 2011). Hopkins and colleagues (2010) have estimated that, in the case of India, the annual value of public subsidies for the education of medical professionals is over $100 million.

Another issue identified in the literature is the case of the use of public healthcare facilities for private foreign patients, limiting their use by the local population (Smith et al., 2011). For instance, in Malaysia, the government has considered selecting some wards or wings in public hospitals so they can be ring-fenced for private foreign patients, increasing the waiting time for services for the local population. As Ormond has argued, this leads to a "two-queue system" that prioritizes "those able to pay over the 'poor'" (2011, p. 253). Thailand is also implementing private wings for private patients in public hospitals, where surgeons might be more inclined to treat private foreign patients over local ones visiting the same facilities (Pocock & Phua, 2011).

The focus of medical travel destinations can also be changing at the expense of the health of their local populations. Research on medical travel has indicated that some countries might be prioritizing the technological development of their medical facilities to provide specialized care to medical travelers, while disregarding the basic needs of the local population such as sanitation, vaccination, and primary care (Bookman & Bookman, 2007; Connell, 2013a). As Ramirez de Arellano has argued, "the fact that the private sector in Bangkok has more gamma knife, computer tomography (CT) scan, and mammography capacity than England is evidence of the distortions that occur in the allocation of resources when these are spent for status symbols rather than to meet local needs" (2007, p. 196).

Some procedures sought in locations away from the patient's place of origin pose particular risks and might raise unique ethical concerns. As outlined earlier, many medical travelers seek care considered illegal in their place of origin. Terminally ill patients travel to the Netherlands and Switzerland, where euthanasia is legal (Connell, 2006). Britain has carried out abortions for patients who are non-residents (Kassim, 2009) and several patients from the UK have traveled to other European countries for fertility treatments not approved by the UK's regulatory body, the Human Fertilisation and Embryology Authority (HFEA) (Kassim, 2009). Some authors have also documented the experiences of patients from Germany who seek fertility treatment in Spain as IVF with egg donation is illegal in Germany (Bergmann, 2011a, 2011b). This type of travel has also been documented in the case of intra-national travel where legislation might vary by region. In the case of Australia, for instance, women from Victoria have traveled to New South Wales, where the law is less restrictive in terms of delivering fertility treatment to single women and women in same-sex relationships (Bennett, 2000; Button, 2000).

Experimental procedures or treatments might also be sought by medical travelers because these are not available in their place of origin. These procedures pose additional ethical concerns as they might be in early testing phases. They might raise questions in relation to the adequate informed consent processes for patients, how to deal with failed attempts and complications (infection being one of the most common ones reported in the literature) (Song, 2010). Stem cell therapies have been highlighted as one example of these types of procedures, with a limited number of clinical trials in operation but over 700 clinics providing these services to traveling patients across the world (Caufield et al., 2012; Einsiedel & Adamson, 2012; Song, 2010).

Follow-ups and the continuity of care are issues highlighted for all treatments/procedures sought by medical travelers (Crooks et al., 2013; Eissler & Casken, 2013; Lunt & Carrera, 2010; Martinez Alvarez et al., 2011; Smith et al., 2011). There are questions about the quality of care that can be delivered to patients when the different healthcare professionals and facilities delivering care are not communicating with each other (or have limited contact in relation to the patient's clinical history or medical notes). Some patients might receive some follow-up care in the destination country/

region, but others might require more longer-term care back in their place of origin. Whose responsibility is it to make sure the patient recovers well? This issue is particularly relevant when patients have complications or where there is evidence of malpractice. Complications that need to be dealt with in the place of origin represent a burden for these healthcare systems as costs are often absorbed by these local hospitals (Crooks et al., 2013). Some doctors in the place of origin have refused to care for patients in these circumstances, leading patients to access care through emergency services (Forgione & Smith, 2007; Mirrer-Singer, 2007). In the case of public healthcare systems, this situation has raised questions around care equity and the fact that public services are being used to fix the problems generated by care received elsewhere (Crooks et al., 2013; Snyder et al., 2011).

Malpractice is tricky from a legal point of view as, in most cases, patients will be subjected to the laws of the place where they received treatment (Kassim, 2009). Countries like India and Thailand have limited malpractice laws (Smith et al., 2011) and many facilities in destination countries have little malpractice insurance coverage (to maintain low prices) (Hopkins et al., 2010). Furthermore, some countries such as Singapore and Malaysia rely on the confession to malpractice of local physicians before compensation can be awarded to the patient (Forgione & Smith, 2007) and other countries such as Thailand do not compensate for pain and suffering (Kassim, 2009).

THE STATE OF ACADEMIC RESEARCH ON MEDICAL TRAVEL

In a recent edited volume on medical travel, Lunt and colleagues (2015) identified three waves of research on medical travel. The first wave was characterized by its emphasis on the novelty of medical travel and focused mainly on describing its main characteristics. Most publications emanated from countries in the Global North and described cases of patients from these countries who sought care in the Global South (Lunt et al., 2015). The second wave had a clearer empirical focus and sought to explore the experiences of patients seeking care abroad. It problematized the terminology used to describe these patient flows (mainly the use of the 'medical tourism' term) and proposed visualizing medical travel as a complex and diverse phenomenon (Lunt et al., 2015). A more nascent third wave of medical travel research continues the trend of empirical studies, but seeks to use these findings to engage in wider theoretical discussions regarding the processes influencing both travel and access/delivery of care (Lunt et al., 2015).

This book responds to this third wave of research as it seeks to demonstrate the contributions of critical perspectives to our understanding of medical travel. In doing so, it tries to expand the scope of the field of medical travel research to include a wide range of mobility forms. This rupture of existing definitions of medical travel is required to invigorate a field of thought that has narrowed the scope of research, much to the detriment of its theoretical development. Medical travel research has tended to neglect the complexity and diversity behind individual migration experiences due to the domination of macro-level approaches. Most studies stem from disciplines such as economics, business, tourism studies, and biomedicine, making the discussion on medical tourism more an issue of health expenditure, insurance coverage, and corporate profit (Connell, 2006; Horowitz & Rosenweug, 2007), and less about the actual experiences of individuals seeking healthcare abroad. The literature produced within the medical sciences tackles similar issues (with the occasional mention of the ethical dilemmas involved in transnational medical attentions) and reproduces financial concerns (Dunn, 2007; Klaus, 2006; Milstein & Smith, 2006; Pafford, 2009).

Anthropological studies have demonstrated that migration is not only structurally organized, but also individually motivated (Low & Lawrence-Zuniga, 2003). As Pieke (1999) has indicated, migration studies have moved from macro analyses of the flows of people to the study of individual migration experiences. This theoretical and methodological shift is based mainly on the recognition of the heterogeneity of migrant groups and the empirical demonstration that the migrant experience is shaped by the characteristics of the individuals who are migrating as well as the structural factors present in arrival areas and places of origin (Fairchild & Simpson, 2004; Fassin, 2005; Lipovec, 2008; Romero-Ortuño, 2004).

Political and economic processes determine the availability of public services and the definition of entitled populations (Baer et al., 2003). The failure to distribute health services evenly among geographical regions sends a clear political message. Biehl (2005) has proposed the concept of "zones of social abandonment" in the attempt to theorize the life-courses of socially unmapped populations. Biehl argues that those that are *abandonados* (abandoned) experience a social death which precedes their biological death (2005, p. 52). He applies Agamben's (1998) concept of "bare life" where the state relies on the use of two main categories in order to maintain its sovereignty: bare life that is common to all animals (zoe) and human experience (bios) (Agamben, 1998). This distinction allows the modern state to exclude or kill specific individuals with impunity because they have been stripped of the bios, that is, their political rights, but remain under the state's control through the zoe (Agamben, 1998, 2005).

If we implement this perspective when analyzing healthcare models, we can see that citizenship (and the rights associated with it) acts as a flexible category, creating limits for certain individuals at specific times (Agamben, 1998). As Appadurai has indicated, the cultural ideologies of the nation-state demand discrimination among different categories of citizens even when they all occupy the same territory (2003, p. 339). The deprivation of healthcare services in certain regions of the country responds to political ideologies and a moral economy of health, factors which are themselves the product of historical processes. Moral economy refers to the economy of the moral values and norms of a given group in a given moment (Fassin, 2005, p. 365). When applied to healthcare delivery, this concept illustrates the beliefs and prejudices associated with certain groups attempting to receive medical attention and the policies used to restrict their access (Farmer, 2003; Fassin, 2005; Whiteford & Whiteford, 2005).

The third wave of medical travel research proposed by Lunt and colleagues (2015) will need to engage closely with the political economy of medical travel drawing from a wide range of critical perspectives. It will need to unpack concepts previously taken for granted within this field of thought and expand definitions of medical travel beyond international travel (focusing more in-depth on intra-regional and intra-national journeys). A fuller understanding of travel, movement, and stasis will be required as these shape patient experience and processes of care delivery. Research will also need to expand beyond the common 'hot-spots' of medical travel, to include a wider range of cultural, geographic, and political scenarios where travel is used to access care.

CHAPTER FOUR

Medical travel at a local scale: An example of intra-national medical travel

Medical travel processes at a global scale, such as those outlined in the previous chapter, are negotiated in local landscapes and reworked to create unique scenarios of care delivery and travel. This is the case for international medical travel as well as intra-national travel. In this chapter, I provide a glimpse into the characteristics of medical travel within national boundaries through the case study of pediatric oncology treatment in Argentina. The chapter situates intra-national medical travel within a longstanding history of healthcare centralization and the unequal distribution of specialized services across the country. It also presents the details of my research and introduces the stories of three families of medical travelers that will feature throughout the book to give texture to the abstract concepts being proposed to study medical travel using a critical (im)mobilities lens.

MEDICAL TRAVEL IN LATIN AMERICA AND THE CARIBBEAN

Despite the boom in medical travel destinations in Latin America and the Caribbean, it remains unexplored as a region in comparison to ASEAN countries or destinations in the Middle East. One of the first countries to develop a medical travel industry was Cuba, but it was upstaged by other destinations that became more popular (Connell, 2013b; Goodrich, 1993). Some research has explored the travel of patients from the US and Europe to destinations such as Costa Rica, Argentina, Mexico, or Brazil for one-off procedures such as cosmetic surgery (Ackerman, 2010; Edmonds, 2011; Viladrich & Baron-Faust, 2014; Warf, 2010). Other countries have earned a spot in the market by offering specialized treatments or procedures such as hair loss therapy and transplants in the Dominican Republic (Stephano, 2012), addiction therapy in Antigua, fertility tourism in Barbados, and prostate cancer and spinal surgery in the Bahamas (Connell, 2013b; Snyder et al., 2013). Some authors have also looked at the flows of patients from Latin America that go to countries such as the US to access specialized care (Crom, 1995; Hadler, 2015). Some of my research has focused on cross-border care, examining the experiences of families who traveled from Bolivia and Paraguay to access medical services in Argentina (Vindrola-Padros & Whiteford, 2012; Vindrola-Padros, 2015).

According to Connell (2013b), this region of the world has four main features that could contribute to the development of a medical travel industry: (1) most countries have tourism-oriented infrastructure and economies, (2) English is the main language in several Caribbean countries, (3) most countries have relatively modern health systems, and (4) diasporic tourism (where nationals who have migrated to other countries return for care) is becoming more common. Challenges are evident in relation to internal competition in the region and competition with well-known international medical travel hot-spots in Asia and some parts of Europe (Connell, 2011a, 2011b, 2013b).

Questions still remain in relation to the development of medical travel in this region of the world. Many countries in Latin America maintain relatively strong public health systems and some countries, such as Argentina, have open migration policies, which means patients from other countries can access free medical attention. What are the features of medical treatment and travel under these conditions? Inequalities in the distribution of services documented in several Latin American countries mean that many patients have to obtain medical services in other areas of the country. How do flows of international patients interact with existing flows of internal medical travelers? The rest of the chapter will describe one case study of intra-national medical travel to begin a much-needed discussion on the particular characteristics of medical care and travel in the Latin American context.

A BRIEF HISTORY OF THE ARGENTINE HEALTHCARE SYSTEM

The healthcare system in Argentina is composed of different types of providers (public, private, non-governmental, related to employment benefits, etc.) in constant competition with each other for healthcare users and facilities. Each responds to the interests of their own sector, leading to fragmentation and disarticulation of care. Even though private insurance companies and healthcare coverage based on employment benefits (referred to locally as *obras sociales*) have suffered a significant expansion, 41.1% of the population does not have any coverage and, thus, relies on the services from the public healthcare sector (INDEC, 2005).

In order to understand the current structure of the healthcare system in Argentina, it is important to briefly go over its history. This history has, to some extent, shaped the distribution of services across the country and generated flows of patients to the capital to access specialized care. Katz (1998) has argued that the Argentine public health system cannot rid itself of its charitable or beneficent past. The author bases this argument on contemporary trends in the administration of public medical services where the provision of medical attention is framed more as a donation than as a universal human right that must be ensured by the state. The universalized, sometimes called socialized, notion of health plays a significant role in current Argentine political rhetoric; but as Katz (1998) and others have argued, in reality, access to medical services is tainted by a historical past, which has constantly (re)configured populations as 'deserving' and 'undeserving' of care. Undeserving populations have tended to be rural areas, mainly in the northern provinces of the country, which have suffered centuries of marginalization and exclusion from public services.

The earliest development of the healthcare system depended on the work of religious organizations and foundations who used charitable donations to provide services to those in need (Thompson, 1995; Vindrola-Padros, 2011). Some of these foundations or societies, like the Beneficence Society (Sociedad de Beneficencia), played an instrumental role in the shaping of future healthcare policies directed at women and children (Nari, 1996; Rodriguez, 2006; Ruggiero, 2004). This society also laid the groundwork for the development of the backbone of healthcare infrastructure, the creation of the first public hospitals in the country (i.e. the Children's Hospital in 1875) and the training of healthcare professionals (mainly nurses, but also involving residencies for doctors) (Armus, 2007; Kohn & Aguero, 1985; Meroni, 1982; Vindrola-Padros, 2009).

The responsibility of the state in the maintenance of the population's health started during the 1930s, as the country experienced an increase in the flows of migrant populations who settled mainly in urban areas. The concept of "social assistance" (that is, the delivery of care by government institutions) became popular and was introduced as an issue of interest to society as a whole (Stawski, 2009, p. 33). The model proposed for the administration of welfare programs was based on the centralization of government institutions and an emphasis was placed on the development of healthcare institutions in the capital of Buenos Aires.

This was the model adopted by the Fundación Eva Peron, an entity founded in 1948, which profoundly marked the change in delivery of health services in Argentina. The organization was directed by Eva Duarte, President Peron's wife, until her death in 1952 and it was in charge of administering large public service facilities (homes, schools, institutes) and the distribution of large sums of subsidies and material donations (Thompson, 1995, p. 55). According to Eva Peron, social justice was a right, a public good that needed to be provided by the state (Thompson 1995, p. 58). The call for the right to health functioned in unison to Eva's discourse on social justice, but was mainly directed by the Minister of Health, Ramón Carrillo. In one of his famous speeches he said, "The problems of medicine as a branch of the state cannot be solved if the sanitary policy is not supported by a social policy" (Carrillo, 1947).

Even though at a discursive level Carrillo's and Peron's approach to healthcare seems similar, disagreements regarding how this universalized model was to be implemented led to a reduction in the number and scale of the transformations of the health system (Katz & Muñoz, 1988; Stawski, 2009). Several institutions were put under the control of Eva Peron, contributing to the increase in centralization of funds and decision-making power (Thompson, 1995). The Fundación decided to spend large sums of money on the creation of complex polyclinic hospitals in big cities that could provide a wide range of services to extensive geographic areas. Carillo, in contrast, believed that the Argentine public health system needed to be decentralized by placing greater attention on making sure remote areas had at least some form of medical attention (Stawski, 2009).

For Carillo, the public healthcare facilities needed to become the backbone of the health system and he sought to distribute material and human resources among existing and new facilities (Califano et al., 1998). Legislative transformations were made and the Constitution of 1949 was the only Argentine Constitution that explicitly proclaimed the right to health (Bidart Campos, 1989). This constitution was revoked in 1956, but the right to health has remained an implicit legal right (Bidart Campos, 1989). Carrillo's advocacy for the right to health and the universalization of coverage did not operate in isolation; it was part of the global recognition of the relevance of public health through the establishment of transnational institutions such as the World Health Organization (Katz, 1998).

The socialization of medicine resulted in one of the largest expansions of medical infrastructure in the country, leading to the creation of facilities for the supply of medical services and the bureaucratic personnel required to administer the health system. As Katz and Muñoz (1988) have indicated, this expansion was carried out in disorganized form, without knowledge of hospital administration, failing to adapt the structure of the hospital to local contexts and sanitary regulations, and was unable to provide the specialist human resources that were required for its administration. A report published by the Pan American Health Organization (PAHO) in 1956 indicated that:

> "The specialty of hospital administration in the Republic of Argentina is found in its infancy, due to the lack of necessary knowledge. Medicine is confused with the hospital, and the doctor with a director or administrator. Technical aspects are mixed with political ones, annulling, many times the first in benefit of the second [...] Due to this fact, the organization renounces, the systems fail, resources are ill-spent, services are inoperable, the performance of the personnel is reduced, etc."
> (Pedroso in Katz & Muñoz, 1988, p. 105)

The lack of planning, disorganization, and superposition of services were also affected by a budgetary crisis, which led Carrillo to announce that "The national sanitary services are insufficiently financed, which is translated into poverty, lack of technical means, bad organization, and, consequently, deficient service [...] The resources of the State have reached their limit, forcing the reduction of public expenditure" (Belmartino & Bloch, 1982). As a response to this situation, different models of patient fee collection were attempted and proposals to decentralize health service provision to provincial facilities entered the political agenda.

DECENTRALIZED PLANNING

The push toward decentralization was not only an idea professed locally, it was spread around the world by transnational organizations. As mentioned earlier, the PAHO had produced an unfavorable report regarding the situation of the Argentine public health system. One of its recommendations for improvement was the transference of the responsibility of public hospitals to each province (Katz, 1998). These measures were followed during the late 1950s and the 1960s, but even though the right over these facilities was passed on to provincial governments, the required technical and financial support did not follow (Katz, 1998, p. 21). As a consequence, the public hospitals around the country started to suffer a long process of deterioration, one that remains even today.

This time period and the decade of the 1970s that followed was an unstable and tragic stage in the history of the country as several democratic governments were intervened by military de facto dictatorships. In the health sector, this was a time when the system of *obras sociales* was consolidated (Belmartino, 2005, p. 132). *Obras sociales* have been defined as "social-welfare programs administered by unions" (Golbert, 2000, p. 239). The creation of the Instituto de Obra Médica Asistencial (IOMA), an *obra social* in charge of providing medical attention to the governmental personnel in Buenos Aires marked the first step in this direction (Belmartino, 2005, pp. 151–152). However, it was not until the approval of law 18.610 in 1970 that the system of *obras sociales* was solidified. This law established, for the first time, the mandatory provision of benefits by the employer and mandatory affiliation, and created the Instituto Nacional de Obras Sociales (INOS) as a regulating agency (Califano et al., 1998; Katz & Muñoz, 1988). The introduction of this third actor in the health sector (in addition to private and public) pluralized the system and neutralized the domination of healthcare provision by the government (Katz & Muñoz, 1988, p. 22).

The private sector had slowly gained ground since the fall of Peron's first era and it gained momentum during Ongania's de facto government from 1966 to 1970. The political forum began to display a discourse of markets for healthcare, outsourcing, and coverage benefits. The representation of medical professionals as servants of the state that had dominated the political sphere in earlier decades was now replaced with descriptions of assets and hiring mechanisms (Katz & Muñoz, 1988, p. 25). The brief return of Peronism from 1973 to 1976 attempted to re-centralize the public health system, but little could be achieved under a regime of political persecution, civil conflict, and genocide. From a political perspective, the situation worsened in 1976 with the military coup that placed Videla in the presidency and would come to represent one of the darkest periods of Argentine history, where nearly 30,000 people disappeared and all areas of public service provision were interrupted and practitioners were persecuted (Wright, 2007, p. 114).

The private sector grew stronger and the medical model changed to have a higher dependency on diagnostic technology and treatment (Katz & Muñoz, 1988, p. 26). The preventive model that represented the roots of the Argentine health system in the 1800s was rapidly replaced by a technocratic curative medical practice. This change certainly mirrored transformations taking place at a global level and was partially enforced by international organizations such as The World Bank and the International Monetary Fund (Belmartino, 2005).

The installation of a democratic government in 1983 revived the struggle for the protection of human rights that had been initiated by several civil society organizations during the last military dictatorship. This historical stage also involved governmental restructuring in the area of public service provision. Measures were taken to reorganize the system of *obras sociales* and to establish a national health coverage system, the PMO (Programa Medico Obligatorio) that will be described later. According to Veronelli and Veronelli (2004), the political decisions made during this period did not portray a real interest in improving the public health system, but were mainly focused on solidifying the processes of privatization that had begun in earlier decades. The decree 9/93 proposed the modification of the system of *obras sociales* in order to allow affiliates to choose their coverage, thus promoting competition among providers and establishing a market exchange of healthcare (Califano et al., 1998, p. 27). The decree 9/93 also established that the *obras sociales* were in charge of paying for the services their affiliates received in public hospitals. This measure was a continuation of the process of decentralization started earlier (1950s) and responded to a new proposal (decree 578/93) of hospital self-regulation where hospitals were granted freedom in the administration of their budgets (expenses, income, salaries, etc.) (Belmartino, 2005, p. 206).

Under this decree, each hospital would negotiate expenses with the *obras sociales* and would administer the income obtained for the provision of services to their affiliates. These measures have certainly created a complex situation of health service delivery and payment where the demand for coverage often falls in the hands of the individual patients and their families. Furthermore, the gap between hospitals located in the capital (with more income) and those in the provinces widened. The 1990s also witnessed the more notable presence of another actor in the system of healthcare, the companies of *medicina prepaga* (prepaid medicine). These companies have been defined by Belmartino as "organizations dedicated to the coverage of private insurance of medical attention that find their market niche among the population with highest income" (2005, p. 218). The companies were present in earlier decades, but it was during this time that they became of interest to local and international investors. The freedom of beneficiaries established before also led many affiliates of the *obras sociales* to seek private insurance with these prepaid providers (Belmartino, 2005, p. 219).

This does not mean that the state suddenly renounced its role as responsible for the health of its citizens, the PMO was designed to establish conditions of equity by demanding mandatory coverage for a series of health conditions. It was designed to protect individuals from the denial of services by insurance companies and to guarantee that the entire population had at least minimal coverage (Belmartino, 2005; Mera & del Castillo, 2000). The creation of the PMO represented a significant step in the maintenance of a universalized model of healthcare, however, in reality, the lack of regulatory capacity of public institutions resulted in the creation of multiple PMOs and the permanence of profound inequalities in the supply of health services (Mera & del Castillo, 2000, p. 47).

THE CURRENT HEALTHCARE SYSTEM

As mentioned before, the healthcare system in Argentina is characterized by a longstanding history of centralization of specialist medical services and fragmented delivery of care across three sectors (public, private, and *obras sociales*). Despite attempts to decentralize care and guarantee the equal distribution of medical services, it is also overwhelmed by profound internal inequalities. In a comparison of 20 Latin American countries, Ugalde et al. (2002) found that Argentina was the country with the highest per capita health expenditures and the second highest in total health expenditures as percentage of GDP (see basic indicators in Table 1). However, there are significant differences when considering access to care, expenditure, and disease incidence at the level of each province (Lloyd-Sherlock, 2002). Tobar and colleagues (2011) found some provinces would spend seven times more of their budget on healthcare. Other studies have reported a high concentration of medical professionals in large cities, where Buenos Aires, for instance, has seven more doctors per person than some of the northern provinces such as Formosa and Misiones (Bello & Becerril-Montekio, 2011). The unequal distribution of mortality has been linked to differences in socio-economic variables as well as differential access to potable water, sanitation, and health services. Recent mapping studies have also pointed to the unequal distribution of medical facilities, healthcare professionals, training, and the development of provincial policies for specific services, such as palliative care (Mertnoff et al., 2017).

Table 1. Basic indicators in Argentina

Total population in 2008	39,745,613
Total population of men in 2008	19,465,305
Total population of women in 2008	20,280,308
PBI per capita (2008)	9647.5
Annual population growth index (1991–2001)	10.1
Global fertility rate (2005–2010)	2.3
Life expectancy at birth for both sexes (2005–2010)	75.24
Literacy rate in the population aged 10 years and older (2001)	97.4
Infant mortality rate by 1000 live births (2008)	12.5
Maternal mortality rate by 10,000 live births (2008)	4.0
Deaths caused by infectious diseases (2009)	13,756
Deaths caused by tumors (2009)	60,117

Source: Ministerio de Salud (2010).

CANCER TREATMENT IN ARGENTINA AND THE NEED FOR MEDICAL TRAVEL

Several researchers have pointed out that pediatric oncology patients accessing care in developing countries have less access to adequate medical treatment and lower survival rates (Arora et al., 2007; Howard et al., 2004) due to the unavailability of treatment in local medical facilities, lack of training of healthcare professionals, the unreliable supply of medications, and delays in initial consultations (Arora et al., 2007; Howard et al., 2004). As a result, pediatric oncology patients arrive with advanced cases of cancer, have to suspend therapies, have a greater probability of relapse, and experience higher rates of death produced by toxicity and infections (Howard et al., 2004; Wagner & Antic, 1997).

Cancer is the leading cause of death (without considering accidents) in children aged between 5 to 15 years in Argentina (Moreno, 2007). Eighty-seven percent of pediatric oncology patients rely on the medical services provided by the public health system (FNDF, 2008). As mentioned earlier, the Argentine public health system guarantees free and universal access to medical attention and treatment for individuals in the country's territory. In the case of cancer, there is no specific legislation for this disease, but patients' rights are discussed under the PMO. This law has suffered transformations through previous years, but one of its main points is that individuals in need of antiretroviral therapy (in the case of HIV/AIDS), oncology treatment, prenatal care, diabetes, among others, must receive 100% coverage of medical procedures and medication. In the case of oncology patients without insurance who are accessing services in public hospitals, all services are provided within public hospitals and the drugs necessary for chemotherapy or hormone therapy are provided through the Oncology Drug Bank (Banco Oncológico de Drogas).

Researchers from different disciplines have critiqued Argentina's lack of policies on cancer, arguing that lack of specificity in terms of diseases is a technique used for avoiding high-quality coverage (Politi, 2001). Some authors have mentioned that national treatment protocols have not been approved due to the fact that they would produce cost elevations (Politi, 2001). As a consequence, policy analysts have spoken of a fragmented, unarticulated, and unequal health system where each province is left to define for itself the budget, infrastructure, and medical personnel available for the treatment of cancer (Abriata & Moreno, 2010; Olaviaga & Maceira, 2007). The impossibility of many provinces to deal with the expenses of cancer treatment and the unavailability of pediatric oncologists in provincial hospitals leads to the referral of child patients to Buenos Aires (Abriata & Moreno, 2010, p. 45). Between 2000 and 2005, 4 out of 10 patients younger than 15 years of age migrated to the main pediatric hospitals of the country, which are found in Buenos Aires (Abriata & Moreno, 2010, p. 45). By 2017, 50% of all children diagnosed with cancer were treated in three main specialist centers, meaning that at least 44% of all diagnosed pediatric cases had to travel outside of their province at least once during their treatment (ROHA, 2018).

In several ways, this movement of patients has become engrained in the daily working mechanisms of public hospitals as a series of formal and informal procedures have been implemented to ensure travel and relocation. In terms of the use of public transportation within Buenos Aires, the law number 2.596 promulgated in 2008 allows individuals with oncology pathologies [defined as treatment extending 3 months] who receive treatment in specialized areas of the hospitals in the state subsector of the city of Buenos Aires to travel free of charge. Casas de la Provincia (Province Houses) are the institutions that provide greater financial support for traveling families (Toziano et al., 2004). Basically, these are institutions that represent each Argentine province in Buenos Aires and provide legal services to individuals from their province, disseminate cultural activities, promote tourism, and assist traveling patients.

The lack of documentation and formal procedures for providing services to oncology patients makes it difficult to analyze how the support varies according to each province. However, an informal survey carried out by FNDF in 2009 indicates that most decisions on the type and length of support provided to patients take place on a case-by-case basis. The procedures behind decision-making appear 'secretive' as no formal documentation is provided. The extent to which each Province House is involved in decisions to support patients varies as some only perform administrative tasks, while others make decisions entirely on their own.

Furthermore, different actors in each province are in charge of determining the type of support available for patients. For instance, in Santa Cruz the cases are reviewed by the Ministerio de Asuntos Sociales (Ministry of Social Issues), while in Neuquén the cases are analyzed by the Subsecretaría de Salud (Secretary of Health) (FNDF, 2009).

In sum, Argentine cancer policies are not addressing the evident inequalities in access to medical services by region, especially for pediatric patients. These inequalities in the distribution of specialized services and the negative perceptions patients tend to have of local services are the main triggers for the somewhat stable flows of patients who travel from different areas of the country to Buenos Aires to access care. Official records of government services available for patients traveling to Buenos Aires (or other provinces) in search of medical attention have not been produced. This last factor does not allow patients and family members to demand government support unless it is offered by hospital staff, government officials, or NGOs focused on patient advocacy, who are familiar with the ways of working of government institutions. In other words, universal access and coverage work well on paper, but have little to do with the negotiations and demands of pediatric oncology patients and their families in relation to treatment and support during travel.

MY ETHNOGRAPHIC RESEARCH OF INTRA-NATIONAL MEDICAL TRAVEL

My ethnographic research on the travel experiences of families seeking oncology treatment in Buenos Aires was shaped by the healthcare context described above. I originally set out to understand the experiences of children and parents obtaining care after a cancer diagnosis, yet the distribution of medical services meant that many of the families I would encounter in Buenos Aires were from outside provinces. This situation opened my eyes to large flows of patients who needed to leave their place of origin and travel to the capital to access care, and the challenges, hardship, and sense of hope associated with these travels. In this section of the chapter, I present how I approached the research and briefly describe the lives of some of the families who shared their stories with me.

FIELDWORK

The fieldwork took place in Buenos Aires, Argentina and was divided into three stages: May–August 2008, May–August 2009 and May–August 2010. On all occasions, the research was carried out in collaboration with Fundación Natalí Dafne Flexer (FNDF), a local non-governmental organization that provides medical and other forms of assistance to pediatric oncology patients and their families. I met families in these facilities and they invited me to accompany them on their journeys throughout the city. Through these journeys, I visited the hotels where they stayed, rode the bus or subway with them, waited in the government facilities where they requested appointments, drugs, and services, and spent time in the places they liked to frequent to have fun.

I used multiple methods to collect data in this study: interviews, four different types of patient drawings, participant observation, and historical and public policy document analysis. I recorded and transcribed 70 interviews (35 with parents and 35 with children), 41 drawings were made by children and parents and I recorded and transcribed their interpretations, I followed ten families (included in the original 35) during the last portion of the fieldwork (May to August 2010) and recorded these observations in the form of fieldnotes, and consulted four historical archives.

The interviews were organized to obtain disease and treatment histories for each patient and children and parents were asked to describe their family's experience with treatment and travel. I asked the child and parent to supply information about the technical details of their diagnosis and treatment (i.e. dates, locations, procedures) as well as the series of events that formed part of their migrant experience. In the cases where the family introduced the topic of obtaining non-medical services such as government subsidies, material donations or financial aid, I asked detailed questions about the processes in place for obtaining these. After going over these details, I asked families more general questions about their ideas toward healthcare in Argentina, their advice for other children/parents in the same situation, and their reflections on how pediatric oncology treatment could be improved.

I combined verbal narratives with the use of visual methods in the form of drawings. Each child was asked to develop four drawings. In the first drawing, the children were allowed to draw anything they wished. The rationale behind this freestyle drawing was to allow the child to become comfortable with the method as well as to provide the child with a mechanism to express issues that had not been considered by the researcher. Next, I asked them to draw scenes of diagnosis and treatment. I left these instructions vague enough to allow the children flexibility in the interpretation of the terms and the expression of their diagnosis and treatment experiences.

I asked both children and their parents to draw visual life course timelines. These timelines translated life history methodology into a visual form. The idea behind using visual timelines was to triangulate this information with the histories collected verbally. The timelines provided insight into the temporal and spatial organization of the families' lives and represented a useful mechanism for understanding shifts in already mobile lives.
I also asked each child to draw the issue or event that had created greatest difficulty for them. I left these instructions vague on purpose. After the drawings were completed, I asked the child to interpret them and recorded these interpretations. The drawings were used to obtain information on specific experiences in the child's life that created changes. They showed the extent to which cancer diagnosis and migration were conceptualized as disruptive life events by the child.

The interviews, timelines, and drawings were combined with participant observation in various settings. The collection of these data focused primarily on the interaction between patients and parents, healthcare professionals, and other relevant actors. I kept careful documentation of the quotidian aspects of life for both children and parents through daily family activity charts. Ten families (included in the original sample of 35 families) were followed through their daily routines. The information collected from these observations provided a connection between the micro level of patient life and action and the macro level of the institutions they frequented. By keeping track of the activities of children and parents in specific areas, I could obtain a greater understanding of how structures constrained movement and influenced treatment experiences without losing track of the ways in which they conceptualized and reconfigured these spaces according to their own ideas, interests, needs, and motivations.

I carried out historical and contemporary document research to understand the transformations that medical treatment in Argentina has undergone through time (specifically in the last 100 years) and analyze the historical background of contemporary public health policies. The historical research focused on the analysis of centralization/decentralization attempts of health services throughout Argentine history and changes in the services provided to oncology patients by the state. I selected these topics because they could provide insight into the current policies, programs, and services directed at pediatric oncology patients.

Another portion of the historical research focused specifically on pediatric medicine and the transformations this sub-discipline has undergone through time. The analyses of the processes behind the constitution of the pediatric subject were important for understanding contemporary doctor-patient relationships and the expected role of the child during long processes of hospitalizations. The meanings associated with children and their rights also determined the design of local and global policies concerning access to healthcare and other forms of well-being.

I collected contemporary health policies to situate the information obtained on individual experiences during medical treatment and travel within a larger context. This involved a review of the laws that demarcate: the right to health, the distribution of medical resources, the provision of government funding to patients for issues that are not directly linked to medical services (i.e. housing, transportation, education), and access to services required to ameliorate the secondary effects of medical treatment (i.e. disabilities, assisted reproductive technologies). I also consulted local and international child policies as well as periodical publications.

DATA ANALYSIS

I transcribed the recordings from the interviews and descriptions of the drawings in Spanish and compiled the field notes from the participant observation into one file. I translated specific quotes to English. I analyzed the content of each narrative in the following ways. The stories served as the base for identifying all of the actors involved in the situations described during the interviews (i.e. doctors, nurses, other parent, siblings, volunteers, etc.)

I identified the main scenes described during the interviews and organized them into categories. It is important to take into consideration that the scenes described by the children and parents were structured by the dynamic of the interview guide which delineated a temporal and sequential arrangement based on biomedical stages (identification of symptoms, diagnosis, treatment, control, relapse, palliative care). However, not all of the participants adhered to this structure and many changed the questions to their liking, skipped stages, critiqued the questionnaire and suggested new questions for its improvement. In other words, even though the narration is heavily influenced by the interview setting and questionnaire, the parents and children played active roles in fashioning a narrative that could represent their lived experiences.

I used the patterns found in the representation of actors and scenes to create a list of codes. Once I created the list of codes, I reviewed the transcripts and coded them with computer software (Atlas.ti). Atlas.ti facilitated the establishment of different types of coding, the comparison of interview transcripts, and the coding of images such as the drawings. I also made a list of the topics that were not discussed to compare the issues that did not form part of parents' and children's stories. I compared the transcripts of all individuals according to these codes in order to select the most frequent topics of conversation and to determine how experiences varied among the participants.

I also used the narratives to map out the journeys of each family, their destination(s), places where they stopped, and any back and forth between Buenos Aires and their place of origin. The salient topics in children's and parents' narratives were then analyzed in relation to the place where the child received treatment, their place of origin, and their type of journey.

I paid attention to the way in which stories were influenced by the spaces where the interviews were conducted. Furthermore, I analyzed the narratives in relation to the larger economic and political context where healthcare is delivered and the biographical background of the narrators (social class, place of origin, gender, age, stage of treatment, and medical prognosis). The analysis of this information followed the model proposed by Gubrium and Holstein (2009) performing a holistic reading of narratives where attention is paid to their content and the circumstances behind their production.

The information collected on the characteristics of each household was instrumental in the process of contextualizing parents' and children's narratives. These data were summarized into brief vignettes on each family and portions of these descriptions were used to understand processes of scene selection. The data collected from the reflections the children and parents made regarding the healthcare system, their experiences accessing medical services, and the advice they would give to other families were analyzed using thematic analysis where the main themes were coded and representative quotes were used to illustrate them.

The drawings were analyzed in relation to the audio-recorded explanations made by the children. These interpretations were also coded by paying attention to the general topic of the drawing. The labels used by the participants when describing the drawings were used as the codes in an attempt to represent their voices more accurately. A comparison of the topics of the drawings and the scenes in the narratives was made to see if there were similarities in the issues expressed verbally and visually. The information collected through participant observation was also transcribed and the content was analyzed using the same codes. These notes were used to situate children's and parents' voices in the relevant context.

THE CHILDREN AND PARENTS WHO SHARED THEIR STORIES WITH ME

I was able to map the journeys of 35 families from areas outside of Buenos Aires whose children were undergoing cancer treatment in four public hospitals in the capital. These hospitals were selected because the families who frequented FNDF's headquarters received treatment in these medical facilities. Only one parent refused to participate in the research project (specifically in the fieldwork that took place from May to August 2010).

Children in different stages of treatment (after diagnosis, during treatment, in remission or control, and in cases of relapse) were asked to participate in order to achieve a better understanding of how perceptions change through time. Participants from different provinces of the country were selected to obtain greater diversity in travel experiences.

Families from 15 different provinces were included in the sample. The highest number of participants came from Provincia de Buenos Aires, Salta, and Entre Rios. The cases of children from Provincia de Buenos Aires (the closest province to Buenos Aires city) that were included were those in which the family had more than 3 hours of travel back home and, therefore, could not commute daily to Buenos Aires to obtain treatment. In terms of distance to the place of origin, the highest percentage of families came from provinces located between 1000 and 1500 kilometers away from Buenos Aires, followed by those less than 500 kilometers away and 500 to 999 kilometers away.

Most of the children included in this study were diagnosed with leukemia (17 children). This corresponds with the distribution of cases at a national level as the latest results from the only pediatric oncology registry in the country, the ROHA (2008), which indicates that the most common type of cancer in children is leukemia (37.1% in 2007) (see also Abriata & Moreno, 2010). Leukemias have an incidence rate of 3–4 per 100,000 children below the age of 15 (Moreno, 2007). Among the leukemias, the most common is ALL (acute lymphocytic leukemia) (ROHA, 2008).

Children receiving treatment in four public hospitals were included in this study. Hospital de Alta Complejidad, Hospital General, and Hospital Infantil are children's hospitals located in the capital of Buenos Aires, while Hospital Policlínico has a polyclinic format and is located in the Provincia de Buenos Aires (all hospital names are pseudonyms). Most of the children in this study were receiving treatment in Hospital de Alta Complejidad.

Children in different stages of oncology treatment were selected. Most of the child participants were receiving some form of medical treatment at the time of the interview. This treatment involved chemotherapy, radiotherapy, and bone marrow transplants. Eleven children were in follow-up stages, that is, they had finished their treatment protocols and were traveling to Buenos Aires on a regular basis for medical surveillance. Six children were interviewed while they were receiving treatment for a relapse and one of these children had traveled to Buenos Aires because of this relapse. One child entered palliative care and another passed away after the interviews were conducted. Children ranging from ages 5 to 17 were included in this study to have a wider range of treatment experiences and determine if the experience of medical treatment varied according to the child's age. More than half of the child participants in this study were younger than 12.

THREE STORIES OF INTERNAL MEDICAL TRAVEL

Each of the families I interviewed had unique experiences of travel and attempts to obtain medical services. I have selected three families who I think exemplify the diversity of experiences in the sense that they differed in relation to region of origin, distance of travel, referral systems, family composition, child diagnosis and prognosis, length of stay in Buenos Aires, and mode of transport.

SEBASTIAN

Sebastian was a shy five-year-old boy who loved to play with cars. He was diagnosed with a tumor of the central nervous system (CNS) and was obtaining treatment in Buenos Aires when I met him. He was from Entre Rios, a province approximately 450 kilometers away from Buenos Aires. Sebastian's story (and the story of his mother) is one of incredible tenacity. His mother would not rest until she knew what was wrong with her child and until she could guarantee he received the best care. She described her initial ordeal as follows:

> "When he was 9 months old, I had him in his play pen and I saw that his head tilted to one side. It was like he had neck pain and his neck was crooked. From then on he did not lift up his neck. I took him to the pediatrician; he did some stimulation, massage, because he said it was a muscular problem. He then had problems with his eyesight, he had an unbearable photophobia. There was no way to keep him with light in the house, with a 25 [watt] lamp, he would cry. The light made his eyes sting. They then told me that he had contagious conjunctivitis.

Well, then he had trouble with food. Everything he ate he aspirated. He choked with a grain of rice. He then walked and lost stability. He would tilt sideways and when he fell, he would hit his head against the ground. One of the women I knew in the hospital told me 'Mom, this is not right because a muscle spasm would have improved in a month or two.' He was worse, and I would go to the hospital every single day. There was a time when I took him to doctors continuously, he saw the pediatrician, traumatologist, neurologist, kinesiologist, ophthalmologist, and none of them could tell me what he had. I would see him get worse at night, he would not react, he would get all purple, he had respiratory arrests, so one night I went, desperate, and told the doctor, 'Sebastian will not survive the night.' Because of this they told me they would perform a scan, I am talking about a year and 3 months of going through all of this.

They brought me here to Lomas de Zamora [located in the province of Buenos Aires] to do the study. When the local hospital went to pick up the results of the study for me, because they do not travel often, it took them 2 months to travel to Lomas de Zamora, but they would not release it, so I had to wait one more month. It took three months for them to give me the results and for me to find out what Sebastian had. When I saw that he could not resist anymore because he would choke and could not eat anything, I changed pediatricians because I saw that he was not improving [...] All of that time they didn't do a study, not one radiography, not one funduscopy. If they had done a funduscopy, they would have seen it [the tumor]. But I never stayed still, I never took steps back. I had trouble with my family, with my husband, because I would tell him 'I'm leaving' and he would ask, 'you're going to the hospital again?' I would see that my child would not improve, and the way that he came to Buenos Aires, he was a completely disabled child because he would not walk, talk or eat."

Sebastian traveled to Buenos Aires with his mom in 2009. He was treated immediately for his CNS tumor and they both remained in Buenos Aires to receive treatment for two years before being able to go back home:

"From one day to the next I had to leave my house, my family, my daughter who was 5 at the time and was practically raised by her grandparents. Two years without seeing her. We would only talk on the phone because of the chemo, you know, his defenses [son's] would lower, his platelets, and we could not leave […] I brought him in with 31,000 platelets only, and the doctor said we couldn't leave. From then on, we didn't go back. Two years without going back."

During one of our conversations, I asked Sebastian's mom to draw a timeline of her life. She decided it would only contain two stages: "this is what happened when it was only him and me getting the treatment, and this is now with our family back together." She explained that Sebastian's illness made her see the world in black and white now. She could summarize her life in relation to the time before and after her child started experiencing symptoms, a time which acted as a disruption of her normal family life.

Sebastian also made a drawing about his treatment. He titled it "Me in the city" (Yo en la ciudad, in Spanish). Even though he appears alone in the drawing, our conversation went over how the loud noises and strange people sometimes scared him. He also mentioned his favorite things to do in Buenos Aires: going to soft-play areas, watching theater plays for children, and frequenting the most enormous toy stores he had ever seen.

Despite being separated from her family for two years, Sebastian's mom has a positive attitude toward her son's treatment. He was responding well to treatment and was not experiencing any of the symptoms that led her to seek care in Buenos Aires. They were living back home and only traveling to Buenos Aires for regular follow-ups. Things were slowly coming together now and she could count on some sense of normality in her daily life. Life would never be the same and there was a constant fear that Sebastian's tumor would come back and his health would deteriorate again, prompting another long trip to Buenos Aires.

CAMILA

Camila was an assertive young girl (14 years old) undergoing follow-up care after completing treatment for AML in Buenos Aires. Camila and her dad traveled from Salta, a province about 1400 kilometers away from the capital. They had relocated temporarily for treatment in Buenos Aires and were now allowed to go back home and travel back regularly for tests and consultations. Camila's dad was her main companion during treatment, and although she missed her mom, she knew her baby brother needed her more.

Camila's leukemia was dismissed as a simple cold, even though her family made recurrent visits to the doctor in their rural town in Salta for over a year. When her health condition worsened and she started suffering hemorrhages, she was referred to a hospital in a larger city in Salta. "It became too much. She had blood dripping out of her nose, her mouth, her ears. We could not wait any longer," Camila's dad explained. She stayed hospitalized in this hospital for weeks and when the doctors could not provide a diagnosis, Camila's dad pressured them into giving Camila a referral to a hospital in Buenos Aires. Camila traveled in an ambulance plane to Buenos Aires and was immediately diagnosed with AML. She remained in Buenos Aires with her dad until she completed her treatment.

Camila now had to undergo regular check-ups in Salta (her province of origin), but when I asked if she would have preferred to carry out her entire treatment in this hospital she said no and explained her answer in the following way:

> "No, the doctor I have there [Salta], if I talk to her, she acts as if I didn't talk to her and she doesn't worry about things. She has this schedule where if I have an appointment at 10, then if I am late, she won't see me. But here [in Buenos Aires] if I am late, she [other doctor] sees me, and she understands why things happen, why I couldn't be there. Over there [Salta], they don't. For example, whenever I go to my house, there is always a strike by the people from there and we tell the doctor that we did not arrive because there was a strike and she doesn't believe us and so my dad has to argue with her."

Camila explained how she had developed a great relationship with her doctors in Buenos Aires and liked visiting them when she traveled to the capital for her regular follow-up appointments. Her dad described the treatment experience in positive terms. They had support from the government to pay for some of the travel expenses and were happy with the care delivered in the hospital. Camila, nonetheless, felt guilty about the impact of her treatment and the need to travel on the rest of her family. She talked about the fact that her dad had to quit his job as caretaker of a farm to travel with her to Buenos Aires. This had negative consequences on the family members who remained in Salta as he was the main income provider. Her mother started baking at home and selling food to workers who would pick crops in nearby fields and her brother, who was 16 at the time, had to quit school to work as a caretaker in another farm.

Camila was adamant that she would finish school and get a 'good job' to help her family out. The continuation of education in Argentina when children need to undergo intensive and long-term treatment is difficult. Not all hospitals have a long-distance education system and not all schools let students study remotely. Camila's dad had requested a special arrangement with the school's head teacher in order to continue with her schoolwork while she was in Buenos Aires. Camila explained this as follows: "My dad explained the problem that I have and all they [the school] require is that I take my medical certificate [...] When I come back I look at my classmate's notes so that I can study for the exams because if I don't have them, then how am I going to study for the exams?" The last time we met, Camila was doing well in school and her family life had gone back to normal. She was still traveling to Buenos Aires for regular appointments, but saw these trips in a different light. "It is easier now," she said, "I actually enjoy coming here [Buenos Aires]."

RODRIGO

Rodrigo, a 5-year-old boy with rhabdomyosarcoma, suffered a relapse during the last phase of the fieldwork. His parents had both been intensely involved with his medical treatment and strictly followed the recommendations of the healthcare professionals involved in his care. When Rodrigo finished his chemotherapy and radiotherapy protocol, he left the hospital with a good prognosis and the family returned to their place of origin, a small town in the province of Buenos Aires (350 kilometers from the capital of Buenos Aires). I met Rodrigo and his family when he was just finishing his treatment and receiving the good news.

As my fieldwork continued, however, Rodrigo's health started to deteriorate. During one of his follow-up scans, the oncologists found that the tumor had grown again and his family relocated once more to Buenos Aires, starting a second, more aggressive, treatment protocol. After his last session of radiotherapy, his family made another trip, this time to San Juan (a province in the northern part of the country) to see a 'healing' priest. When I asked his mother why they made this decision, she replied "We figured it couldn't hurt. When your son is ill, you will try everything in this world to heal him."

In many ways, Rodrigo's story is framed by a family's desperate search to save the life of the child. The emotional labor and exhaustion of his parents was welded on their faces. Rodrigo's mom shed tears every time we would talk about her child. This became an internal joke between us, where we would take tissues out of our pockets when we saw each other and wave them in the air (signaling we were ready for any tears that might come our way). Giggling, we would put them back in our pockets. Despite her palpable emotional struggle, she remained strong and hopeful even after the doctors told her there was nothing else they could do to save the life of her little boy.

Rodrigo passed away a few weeks after my fieldwork ended. I gave Rodrigo's mom a call after the burial and, while she was overwhelmed with pain, she had set her mind to improve the care delivered to children in the region. She was working with her husband to raise awareness of the aspects of care that could be improved. They both valued the care their child received in Buenos Aires and would often say this was the only place in the country where children could obtain high-quality treatment. Nonetheless, they were also critical of some of the actions of the doctors, the state of the facilities and the information provided to parents.

Rodrigo's dad remembered how he felt he needed to control his child's treatment protocol, "they were closing one of his tubes and instead of closing the one with the drug, they closed the one that hydrated him. That is why we would keep a photocopy of the chemo details. We actually had control over the mezna, because the nurses would forget. They would tell us to remind them!" Rodrigo's parents trained themselves to 'detect signs of alarm and care for the child in specific ways,' so they could act as advocates for their child. They knew not all parents could do this and as a result, many mistakes were made in the delivery of care to the children. Even though there was nothing else they could do for their child, Rodrigo's parents were determined to improve the care delivered to other children, particularly those who, like them, had traveled from other provinces to Buenos Aires to access care.

CONCLUDING THOUGHTS

In order to fully understand the complex processes involved in medical travel, it is important to explore individual experiences of seeking care away from home. A localized focus allows us to visualize how the historical background of healthcare systems can shape the current distribution of services and patients' ability to access treatment in their place of origin. Argentina is one example of how the longstanding history of centralization of specialized care and underdevelopment of provincial services have contributed to steady flows of patients traveling to the capital to obtain care. The stories presented in the chapter demonstrate how individual families respond to this medical service infrastructure and build their own care trajectories. Important issues such as the tensions between structure and agency, the emotional labor of medical travel, and the imagined notions of the opportunities treatment away from home can afford all emerge from their stories. These dimensions will be explored in detail in the following chapters.

CHAPTER FIVE
Medical travel infrastructures

The critical (im)mobilities framework places considerable emphasis on the concept of infrastructures, understood as the objects, roads, networks, institutions that can both facilitate and constrain movement (Korpela, 2016). It is useful for understanding the wide range of actors and processes involved in enabling and restricting medical travel at local and global scales, that is, the visible and hidden actors, norms and relationships that operate to (re)produce the flows of traveling patients. In this chapter, I will explore the structures and processes that frame medical travel at local and global scales, as well as the ways in which these are negotiated by social actors. I cover evident infrastructures such as state regulation and bilateral agreements for intra-national travel, cross-border care and international travel, but also focus on more elusive and hidden infrastructures in the form of informal actors and brokers. The purpose of the chapter is not to present an exhaustive list of all of the actors and structures involved in medical travel, but to identify the additional layers of inquiry the concept of infrastructures can generate for our study of medical travel.

GLOBAL INFRASTRUCTURES

As several authors have argued, in many cases, medical travel has emerged as a project of the state. Political leaders from around the world have argued that this industry has the potential to make a contribution to the development of health services in their countries, making new specialties and technologies available to the local population (Hopkins et al., 2010; Snyder et al., 2013). A common argument is that this type of enterprise generates financial profit for the country which then spills over into the public health sector, improving the lives of the lowest social classes (Hopkins et al., 2010; Helble, 2011). This represents a shift in many countries from viewing health as a universal right, to seeing it as a commodity and those requiring services as clients (Ackerman, 2010; Whittaker et al., 2010).

In other words, the medical travel industry can be seen by government authorities in destination countries as a source of financial profit and an extension of local models of care-seeking to privatize health services. As

Ormond has argued: "without negating the impact of 'medical tourism' on destinations, in framing it as an external 'innovation' or 'invasion,' we risk not paying sufficient attention to the complex political contexts that have enabled 'medical tourism' and the selective harnessing of patient-consumer flows to flourish in particular places" (2011, p. 256). These flows require the development of different levels of infrastructure, ranging from legal regulation to medical and non-medical facilities designed to provide services to incoming patients and their families.

In the case of medical travel, regulation can be associated with the accreditation of institutions providing care, the registration of individuals attempting to obtain medical treatment away from home and the monitoring and prosecution of cases of malpractice. Different forms of global infrastructures, such as regulatory frameworks, can work to the advantage of patients using medical travel to bypass prohibition of certain procedures back home, but can also leave patients legally unprotected if complications arise (Bergmann, 2011a, 2011b; Whittaker, 2010). However, regulation is a difficult issue to address in medical travel as global regulators such as the World Trade Organization (WTO) tend to focus on increasing access to international trade and not on protecting patients from exploitative practices (Whittaker, 2010).

As outlined in Chapter 3, accreditation has been identified as a potential mechanism to make sure patients are receiving an adequate quality of care, yet this is not standard practice in all medical travel destinations (Smith et al., 2009). While reflecting on their findings from a study of accreditation of fertility clinics in Argentina, Smith et al. (2009) argued that 'non-accredited clinics have total discretion over how to run their clinics and which services to offer, and they are free from official oversight' (Smith et al., 2009, p. 66). This raises concerns about responsibility and accountability if procedures go wrong. As several authors have argued, there is a need at a global level to identify the main areas of responsibility, and mechanisms for regulation and monitoring of the industry to protect those involved from potential harm (Whittaker, 2010, 2011). A critical (im)mobilities framework can allow us to visualize how these infrastructures facilitate and shape medical travel at a global scale and how they adapt (or not) in cases of malpractice.

These mechanisms of regulation as well as the different layers of infrastructure presented in the rest of the chapter could be easily explained by Inhorn's concept of global assemblage in medical travel. Drawing from the work of Collier and Ong (2005), Inhorn applies the concept of global assemblage (defined by Ong, 2005, p. 338, as a "contingent ensemble of diverse practices and things that is divided along the axes of territoriality and deterritorialization"), to her study of reproductive medical travel to allude to the relationship between localized travel and larger political and economic structures (2015, p. 22). An important aspect of the concept of assemblage is the fact that it is always "heterogeneous, contingent, unstable, partial and situated" (Collier & Ong, 2005, p. 12). It can encompass biomedicine, technoscience, international flows of people and body parts, systems of administration and regulation, commerce, and national healthcare and tourism infrastructures (Inhorn, 2015).

THE CREATION OF LOCAL INFRASTRUCTURES FOR CARE DELIVERY

Several ethnographies have explored the growth of medical travel industries across the world, arguing that medical travel is producing new forms of healthcare and transforming existing healthcare infrastructures (Vindrola-Padros, 2015; Whittaker & Chee, 2015). In their study of international hospitals in Thailand, Whittaker and Chee (2015) argue that the boom of the medical travel industry is in part due to the ability to redeploy tourism and service infrastructures already present in the country. One aspect of this infrastructure redeployment has been the transformation of hospitals into luxurious hotel-like facilities. These hospitals operate as 'hybrids,' maintaining some characteristics of hospitals and adopting others from hotels (Whittaker & Chee, 2015). These 'international hospitals' have served their purpose well by attracting large numbers of wealthy patients, but this duality also creates tensions for patients and staff, who must negotiate comfort (i.e. private bedrooms with no visible medical equipment) with the delivery of safe care (i.e. the need to maintain hygienic practices) (Whittaker & Chee, 2015). Another point of tension are perceptions of the hospitals as both international and local, where certain elements of Thai culture might be exacerbated or minimized depending on the circumstances and where international patients interact with local ones in multi-layered and unequal healthcare environments (Whittaker & Chee, 2015).

Another aspect of the development of local medical infrastructures that has been explored is the training and development of the workforce capable of delivering services to international patients. In an interesting analysis of the rise of Brazil as a destination for cosmetic surgery, Edmonds (2011) draws our attention to the practices used locally to increase the attractiveness of the surgical specialty. He reflects on the ethical implications of a healthcare system that uses working-class patients in public hospitals to train surgeons that will then provide high-quality services to patients from wealthy nations. The public hospital setting allows surgeons to operate on high volumes of patients and have the freedom to innovate in terms of surgical techniques (Edmonds, 2011). Working-class patients are 'the human material necessary for scientific training' for surgeons that are then used to address international demand for surgical services (Edmonds, 2011, p. 301).

From the point of view of a critical (im)mobilities framework, a prominent theme that emerges from the literature is the reproduction of existing inequalities in the delivery of care and the negative impact of medical travel on the poorest and most marginalized sectors of society. Some research has indicated that international medical travel tends to escalate the cost of healthcare for local populations (Saniotis, 2007), drains scarce resources such as capital, technology, and personnel from public medical facilities (Chen & Flood, 2013), and shifts the allocation of resources from primary to tertiary care (Alsharif et al., 2010; Chen & Flood, 2013; Saniotis, 2007). The increase in demand for services by medical travelers allows clinical facilities to charge more in private hospitals, but also impacts public hospitals as personnel, space, and equipment in these facilities might also be used for private medical travel cases (Snyder et al., 2013).

A detailed analysis of how these infrastructures, in the form of regulations, facilities, and staff, are delivered and experienced by a different group of actors sheds light on the heterogeneity of medical travel processes and experiences within the confines of similar material structures. It can also draw our attention to the processes and mechanisms required to perpetuate systems of care delivery that favor the medical needs of some patients over others.

THE FACILITATION OF MEDICAL TRAVEL

Medical travel facilitators have also received attention in the medical travel literature. While focusing mainly on the patient-provider relationship, Dalstrom (2013) identified three different types of medical travel facilitators operating in the delivery of care to US citizens in Mexico: (1) full service facilitators (providing comprehensive services including visas, transportation, physicians, medical facilities, post-operative care and translators), (2) referral service facilitators (connecting patients to a medical provider and other limited services around transportation and scheduling appointments), and (3) individual service facilitators (providers who directly market their services to patients).

Dalstrom (2013) argued that despite slightly different practices, medical travel facilitators relied on the blending of professionalism and mimetic association to gain credibility. An important component of this aspect of credibility was related to the facilitator's capacity to act as a cultural broker (Dalstrom, 2013). This broker role entailed translating aspects of Mexican culture into terms familiar to US citizens, but it also involved the desire to achieve some form of cultural similarity. In other words, medical travel facilitators worked hard to create an image of US-style healthcare delivery in Mexico, so medical travelers would feel more comfortable. Examples of this process of mimetization were the use of the English language in clinical settings and other places frequented by medical travelers, developing links with US 'brands' of healthcare (e.g. Mayo Clinic), and underscoring the homogeneity of medical practice (Dalstrom, 2013).

While some authors have defined medical travel facilitators as intermediaries connecting patients with providers (Dalstrom, 2013), the evidence in the literature indicates that facilitators often take on additional roles and are normally in charge of arranging care for patients, travel options, accommodation, concierge services, travel for touristic purposes, translation, etc. (Whittaker et al., 2010; Whittaker & Speier, 2010). In many ways, they are responsible for what Ackerman (2010) has referred to as the carework of medical travel, or the business of transforming and tending the bodies of travelers. In her study of cosmetic surgery tourism in Costa Rica, Ackerman (2010) identified a wide range of actors responsible for this carework through complex webs of local clinics, luxurious guest houses or residences, and small companies (see also Warf, 2010). The guest houses were particularly important as these not only provided accommodation, but also offered "meals, dressing changes, medication reminders, and maternal ministrations of their *dueñas* (women owners)" (Ackerman, 2010, p. 406). The guest houses, therefore, acted as a fusion between hotels and clinics, taking on some of the caring tasks normally carried out in clinical contexts.

An important part of facilitation is carried out virtually (see, for instance, Cormany & Baloglu, 2011; Lunt & Carrera, 2010; Penney et al., 2011; Viladrich & Baron-Faust, 2014). In a study of medical travel agency (MTA) websites using ethnographic content analysis, Sobo et al. (2011) explored the role of these agencies in promoting medical travel to consumers in North America. They identified a series of assumptions of medical travel consumers reproduced by these companies, such as their desire for 'world-class' care and luxury at low cost, as well as the need to feel in charge of their care while also being cared for by someone else (Sobo et al., 2011, p. 130). The authors argue that the discourse used in these websites creates a structural frame that shapes the desires and actions of both medical traveler and providers (Sobo et al., 2011) and specific 'types' of medical travelers are created and reproduced as a consequence.

The role of online intermediaries has also been explored through online communities. In her analysis of reproductive medical travel in the Czech Republic, Speier (2011) highlights various forms of online brokers, including: websites, blogs, and online support groups. All of the couples included in the study had established contact and stayed connected through blogs and online support groups. The strong role they played in the selection of clinics and services led Speier (2011) to represent online communities as a site of 'patient-consumer activism,' acting as a platform for sharing information and advice, but also capable of shaping patient demand (affecting the business of facilitation companies and clinics).

'HIDDEN' AND INFORMAL ACTORS

Informal actors such as friends, family members, and members of the community have been included in research as a way to explore why and how patients engage in medical travel. Kangas (2007) explored the role of social gatherings in Yemeni patients' desire to travel abroad for treatment and their selection of medical travel destinations. These same-sex gatherings were used to share stories of successful procedures obtained in another country and the details of how journeys could be arranged (Kangas, 2007). They created a sense of potential cure, hope, that functioned as a nuanced trigger and reproducer of patient flows (Kangas, 2007).

Two ethnographies of medical travel in Argentina (my research and one by Eugenia Brage) have also highlighted the role of families and community members in searching for medical services in another location (Brage, 2018; Vindrola-Padros, 2011). Both studies focused on internal medical travel and highlighted the role of community perceptions of local care and stories of friends or relatives who had to travel to the capital of Buenos Aires to obtain 'high-quality' medical services. I argue that negative experiences with local healthcare professionals, examples of successful treatment delivered in Buenos Aires (transmitted by close friends and relatives) and the desire to do everything possible to obtain high-quality care for their ill children, enabled the creation of regular flows of families from outside provinces to Buenos Aires. When traveling families came back to their communities, they shared their stories of life in the big city and, in most cases, the excellent care they received, leading others to plan their own journeys to Buenos Aires.

Research on medical travel also points to the existence of other actors that are part of this infrastructure, but have thus far remained 'hidden.' For instance, in the case of reproductive medical travel, Bergmann has urged us to look beyond the 'evident' actors involved and instead focus on analyzing "the complex constellation of travelling users, mobile medics, sperm and egg donors, locally and globally operating clinics, international standards, laboratory instruments, pharmaceuticals, biocapital, conferences and journals, IVF internet forums and differing national laws" (Bergmann, 2011a, p. 283). This could mean expanding the focus of research from localized hospitals providing care to medical travelers to complex webs of local and global actors that form part of the medical travel infrastructure. Medical travel facilitators, brokers, and other types of intermediaries work to produce medical travel infrastructures, yet these infrastructures are maintained and transformed through interactions with medical travelers who have their own interests, demands, and ideas of what it means to receive care elsewhere.

The focus on hidden actors could also mean considering more informal ways of securing care by participating in medical travel to obtain services that are illegal. The term "rogue medical tourism" has been used to define access to "a medical technology or procedure, which is unavailable because the government has decided to ban or not legalize the intervention" (Cohen, 2015; Hunter & Oultram, 2010). The prohibition of the intervention or procedure could be due to concerns about its safety, lack of evidence regarding its effectiveness or doubts raised about its moral acceptability (Hunter & Oultram, 2010). Some authors have explored strategies to deliver this type of illegal care to patients in covert ways, such as through the use of ships (with medical facilities) situated offshore to take advantage of international shipping laws (English et al., 2005; Hunter & Oultram, 2008).

INFRASTRUCTURING

An underlying theme, though not explicitly mentioned in medical travel research, is the ways in which the medical infrastructures presented earlier in the chapter are constantly reconfigured. Merriman has presented the value of the concept of infrastructuring, arguing that the "affective power of infrastructures extends far beyond their immediate physical bounds, and that infrastructures are in constant process – both socially and materially – requiring physical maintenance, gathering meanings and generating atmospheres" (2016, p. 87). The performative nature of infrastructures allows us to see these processes as never complete and in a state of transience (Lin et al., 2017; Star, 1999).

Some authors have given a historical background to current processes of medical travel, pointing to the factors that have played a role in the expansion of this industry. For instance, Aizura (2010) has argued that the boom in medical travel for gender reassignment surgery (GRS) in Thailand was partially due to the improvement of medical care in Bangkok due to expatriate demand. This existing infrastructure was then adapted to suit the needs of traveling patients seeking procedures such as GRS. The processes for delivering GRS and the patient cohort also changed through time, with a market opening for Europeans and North Americans in the 1990s, and then other Asian countries in the early 2000s (Aizura, 2010). The medical travel industry changed to adapt to this demand, with more surgeons trained to carry out the procedure and more facilities designed to care for recovering patients (Aizura, 2010).

Ackerman (2010) presents a similar picture in the case of cosmetic surgery in Costa Rica, where medical travel emerged through an informal web of local clinics and residences. The changes in the country's healthcare landscape in the late 1990s, with the adoption of neoliberal policies and privatization, led to the creation of large and luxurious private hospitals capable of caring for patients from abroad (Ackerman, 2010). The development of other forms of tourism (e.g. ecotourism), also led to changes in the medical travel industry. Networks and institutions solidified and diversified, creating a sophisticated web of private clinics and high-end guest houses (Ackerman, 2010).

Another interesting example of infrastructuring lies with the role of online communities in the shaping of the medical travel infrastructure. When patients organize themselves as a collective, their voices and previous experiences of medical travel can have a tangible effect on the demand and delivery of services (Speier, 2011). For instance, negative reviews of particular medical facilitators or clinics can have an impact on the site selection of patients considering medical travel, the type of procedure they want to undergo and the residence they will select for their recovery (Bergmann, 2011a; Speier, 2011). This patient demand produces shifts in the medical travel market, with some providers going out of business and others experiencing business growth (Speier, 2016).

In addition to the ways in which medical travel infrastructures have changed through time, medical travel research has explored how infrastructures are negotiated on a daily basis. Kangas (2007, 2010) questions the stereotype of affluent travelers seeking luxurious holidays and medical procedures abroad and describes the experiences of medical travelers who endure great hardship to afford the high costs of travel and medical treatment.

The patients in Kangas' (2007, 2010) ethnography sold animals, cars and compiled great debts in their search for a potential cure for their loved ones. They overcame local structural barriers to gain access to medical resources.

My work in Argentina found many cases of families whose medical travel was not facilitated by anyone, in the sense that they were not formally referred to medical professionals in the capital of Buenos Aires and had no support once they arrived (Vindrola-Padros, 2011). When their child's health turned for the worst, they packed their bags and left in search of a cure. This was the case of internal travelers as well as families from nearby countries who devised their own systems of cross-border care (Vindrola-Padros & Whiteford, 2012). "I just grabbed our things and got on a bus with her," said Eulalia when describing her first trip to Buenos Aires, "I didn't even think about what I would do when I arrived to the city. I went straight to the hospital and she was admitted. I figured it out as we went along, getting some housing, learning which buses to take and where to get her medication." These experiences and those described by Kangas (2007, 2010) shed light on the importance of considering individual agency within the concept of infrastructure and the various ways in which individuals bypass established models of care to seek the services they desire. For these patients, borders became pliable and porous as they made their way to the capital to access treatment.

An important aspect of our focus on the dynamic nature of borders is the fact that it allows us to theorize borders even if these are not the dividing lines of nation-states. In other words, when we abandon static notions of 'the border' and focus instead on bordering processes, we are able to think about political, economic, and sociocultural boundaries and delineations occurring at multiple scales (Green, 2013; Rumford, 2006). As Brambilla has argued, we need to dis-locate and re-locate borders, but also reflect on "the multiplication of border forms, functions and practices through their distribution and proliferation in a variety of social and political arenas, which determine a progressive movement of borders from the margins to the center of the political sphere" (2015, p. 15). These notions of borders as practices are particularly helpful in our examination of internal medical travel as we are able to see the multiple shifting forms of borders patients cross, rework, and (re)conceive when traveling for care.

CONSTRAINED JOURNEYS

An important gap in our understanding of the constraining role of medical travel infrastructures has to do with the fact that most research has focused on the experiences of patients who are able to secure services in another location. This limits our understanding of those who try to seek care elsewhere, but fail. When are borders porous (as outlined above) and when are they rock solid? What are the insurmountable barriers preventing those who need treatment from obtaining it away from home? The critical (im)mobilities framework, with its focus on the role of infrastructures in restraining movement and recognizing the different capacities of individuals for mediating these barriers, could help us answer these questions.

CONCLUDING THOUGHTS

The concept of infrastructure commonly used in mobility studies represents a useful tool to think with and about medical travel. Infrastructures can be material and symbolic, are constantly negotiated and in transformation. The infrastructures of medical travel are highly complex and operate at multiple scales (from policies to informal actors). These infrastructures change through time as medical travel industries develop, but processes and services are also reconfigured on a daily basis by active patients seeking care.

The limiting nature of infrastructures is a dimension that warrants further attention as most research presents examples of successful cases of medical travel. Greater attention needs to be placed on the experiences of patients' imagined possibilities of medical travel (explored in more detail in Chapters 6 and 7) and failed attempts at securing medical services far from home. Another important area to explore is the heterogeneity of medical travelers and their differing capacities for negotiating infrastructures. Infrastructures are not experienced in the same way by everyone, so attention needs to be paid to the characteristics of medical travelers and their unique experiences of travel, as these could point to important processes of infrastructuring. These different experiences of medical travel are the focus of the following chapter.

CHAPTER SIX

Differential medical travel experiences and possibilities

The common use of 'medical tourism' as a blanket term to explain all experiences of medical travel has had a detrimental effect on our understanding of the diversity of experiences of treatment and travel (Whittaker et al., 2010). Various critiques of this concept have already been presented in Chapter 1, but it is important to highlight that as a result of this concept, most of the research carried out on medical travel has focused on international travel and travel for one-off procedures. This means that the experiences of patients seeking care for complex and long-term care and life-sparing treatments, and those traveling within countries have remained largely unexplored.

In previous publications, we have critiqued the limited nature of this body of work and have proposed using the concept of medical travel to explore a wider range of both travel and treatment experiences (Vindrola-Padros, 2015; Vindrola-Padros & Brage, 2017). This would entail considering travel within countries (crossing states, provinces, or regions) as well as more local forms of travel (i.e. within provinces or regions). All forms of mobility require material and symbolic arrangements, and all forms of movement have meaning. Therefore, more local forms of travel can also make contributions to our study of medical travel processes. An important question for us to answer then is: how do experiences and meanings of travel and care vary according to the type of travel (whether international or local), characteristics of the journey, treatment, place of origin, destination, and characteristics of traveling patients and carers?

The purpose of this chapter is to unpack homogenous representations of medical travel and point to the diversity of medical travel practices and experiences. I have reviewed some of the medical travel research through the lens of the concept of differential mobility empowerments used in the critical (im)mobilities framework. This concept seeks to bring power relations to the forefront of analysis by considering that not all who want to move are able to do so (or are able to move in the way they want to). Therefore, mobility can be considered a form of capital, a resource, that in the case of medical travel is often required to improve well-being or even save lives, but a resource that is not equally accessible to everyone.

MEDICAL TRAVEL POSSIBILITIES

This chapter begins with an analysis of the imagination, as imagined notions of potential travel have a direct impact on individual's care-seeking and travel-seeking practices. As Speier has argued for the case of fertility tourism, "there are symbolic and ideological underpinnings to fertility treatments and tourism; both entail imagination filled with promises" (2016, p. 46). The imagination plays a role as the motivator for travel (Speier, 2016), and in the case of Speier's work, this motivation was guided by anticipating the success of reproductive treatment and couples' capacity to fulfill their desire of parenthood. The imagination was fueled by images couples viewed on the websites of medical travel companies, the experiences of other medical travelers, and their own ideas and expectations of what it would mean to become a parent (Speier, 2016).

Song (2010) explores the role of the imagination in similar fashion, arguing that imagined notions of journeys and destinations motivated patients to initiate a quest for a cure. For Song, the imagination should not be considered at an individual level, but, instead, travel should be visualized as "collective journeys of the imagination," where meaning is shared by travelers and generates a new mode of social relatedness (Song, 2010, p. 387). For Kangas (2010), the visible results of other patients who sought care away from home played a more prominent role in the imagined journeys of the Yemeni patients she interviewed (and their decision to seek care elsewhere), than the recommendations to avoid travel made by Yemeni doctors. In her exploration of return migration for reproductive care, Inhorn (2011) uses the term 'diasporic dreaming' to highlight the attachment Middle Eastern expatriates felt to their home countries and how this feeling acted as a 'pull factor' in their decision to travel to seek care.

The imagination, however, does not include the same potential scenarios for everyone. Salazar (2011) has argued that imagined possibilities are shaped by political, economic, and cultural processes that determine what is available or possible for certain individuals. How can you decide to travel for care if you cannot see this as an alternative for you? The families I worked with in Argentina who had traveled from Bolivia and Paraguay to access pediatric oncology treatment for their children often talked about the amount of time it took them to decide to travel. An important factor influencing this decision was their perception that they would not be able to obtain care in Argentina. The specialized centers in Buenos Aires remained a distant imagined possibility that might have never become a reality unless close family and friends encouraged them to cross the border and give it a try.

When the imagination is taken into consideration in research on medical travel, it is often to understand how travel is shaped by ideas of the travel destination, care delivery or life after medical travel. Considerable work needs to be done now to understand those imagined possibilities that are never enacted. What happens with those journeys that are visualized, dreamed about, but never become a reality? How do these imagined journeys influence those that are lived? As we saw in Chapter 2, the critical (im)mobilities framework places an emphasis on the need to consider instances of staying still as meaningful and capable of shaping human experience. These journeys that remain in the imaginary can be a window into these feelings of stillness or stuckness normally analyzed as part of the concept of immobility. These feelings of stillness will shape perceptions of care and future attempts to travel.

CONSUMER CHOICE?

A considerable amount of ethnographic work on medical travel engages with the question of the role of 'choice' in medical care. Dalstrom (2013) has argued that the 'logic of choice' (Mol, 2008) permeates the discourse on medical travel, where patients are seen as being capable of selecting the type of healthcare they want. Speier (2011, 2016) represents medical travelers as consumers shopping for discount treatments. They researched different treatment options, international providers and talked to other patients, or consumers, who had received these services (Speier, 2011). Bergmann (2011a, 2011b) is also captivated by the agency of German medical travelers seeking reproductive technologies in Spain and the Czech Republic and underscores how their agency allows them to circumvent strict regulation on egg donation in Germany.

Even though these authors problematize the concept of choice to some degree, if we only looked at these stories of medical travel, we would be interpreting processes of medical travel as elective, and in some cases, financially viable processes. Kangas (2011) has argued that if we focus on stories of wealthy patients traveling to extravagant locations, we miss the suffering that motivates and permeates travel. We dehumanize travel and treatment by only considering medical travel as "a choice" (Kangas, 2011, p. 330).

Perhaps the concept of stratified care is more helpful in uncovering the power dynamics at play. The concept of stratified care is mainly used in the work on fertility tourism carried out by Whittaker and Speier (Speier, 2016; Whittaker & Speier, 2010). These authors draw from Ginsburg and Rapp's (1991) concept of 'stratified reproduction,' which recognizes that some categories of people are empowered to reproduce, while others are not. The wealthy elite are normally privileged in the process of reproduction (Whittaker & Speier, 2010; Inhorn, 2015), and medical travel intensifies stratification as not everyone will be able to afford travel, accommodation, and assisted reproductive technologies away from home.

Examples of stratified care are seen outside of travel for assisted reproductive technologies (ARTs) as well, where treatments and therapies are only available to those who can afford them and travel to access care. An important point has also been raised when looking at medical travel from the point of view of medical travel destinations. The expansion of the medical travel industry in some locations has meant that public hospital facilities normally used by local patients might be used to treat foreign patients (Vindrola-Padros, 2015). The care delivered is normally not the same quality for both groups of patients and facilities might be differentiated to provide foreign patients with a more luxurious service (Whittaker et al., 2010; Vindrola-Padros, 2015). These inequalities raise important ethical questions about the factors underlying this differential access to care (Vindrola-Padros, 2015; Whittaker & Speier, 2010).

Another manifestation of stratified care is found when considering internal medical travel. If we only consider medical travel as the product of consumer choice, we run the risk of not acknowledging that the reason why many patients travel for care is due to the lack of services or low quality of services in their local area. Under the label of 'patient choice,' we might not be able to conceptualize the fact that, to some extent, some patients might not have any other choice but to travel to save their lives. The concept of stratified care allows us to explore the inequalities in the distribution of medical services, identifying the different types of choices available to patients and their families, and how they might negotiate these structural barriers on a daily basis.

In my research on the experiences of children traveling from different parts of Argentina to the city of Buenos Aires to access treatment, most patients and parents left their place of origin because care was not available locally or they perceived local care to be inadequate. If parents wanted to save the life of their child, they had no other choice but to travel to the specialist centers in the capital. However, the way in which they made this choice, and other perhaps smaller choices, depended on the circumstances of the family (their connections in Buenos Aires, support back home, family characteristics, employment, financial situation, education), their local province (support programs for traveling families), and the local hospital (if the hospital made a formal referral to a hospital in Buenos Aires and provided information to parents on treatment and travel). All of these factors pointed to the importance of considering the different components of medical travel journeys, how these vary by patient or family and how they change through time. The complex nature of decision-making also leads us to problematize the concept of 'choice,' questioning if medical travel is a 'choice' in the first place, and, if so, who makes the choice and why.

FUNDING THE JOURNEY

Surprisingly, not a lot of research goes into the details of the logistics of medical travel. The limited research that has focused on these more mundane aspects of seeking care away from home has pointed to the notable amount of arrangements that must be made before a patient, and potentially a carer, engages in medical travel. The fact that this burden, which normally falls on the patient's family, is unexplored means that we still have a considerable amount of work to do in order to understand the complexities of medical travel experiences and how these might vary by social class, gender, location, etc.

Kangas (2007) does an excellent job highlighting the financial implications of travel. While some patients travel to seek cheaper medical treatments, many others need to endure great financial pressures to travel and relocate temporarily. Kangas (2007) presents stories of patients selling belongings such as cars, farm animals, houses, and jewelry to cover the costs, or borrowing money and incurring great debts. She also mentions that several families had unexpected costs while abroad, thus requiring additional funds from their families. According to her, "the financial dimensions of treatment abroad extended the resources and obligations of families and the state beyond local borders" (Kangas, 2007, p. 300). These obligations are not only pertinent to sending money to family members while they are away, but also covering employment and non-paid labor (i.e. childcare and housework) back home.

The stories shared by the parents I interviewed in Argentina, brought to light the weight of these obligations. Sebastian's family had to sell many of their possessions to pay for the trips to Buenos Aires to access care. Care was available for Sebastian at the local hospital in Entre Rios, but after his CNS tumor was confused with a muscle spasm, his mother could not envision taking her child for treatment anywhere else, but to Buenos Aires (where they delivered "excellent care"). Sebastian's mom described their situation as follows: "from one day to the next I had to leave my house, my family. I sold my car, my motorcycle, my husband is a plumber and he sold his tools. He only kept the ones he really needed for work. He was the only one bringing money home, so we needed to make sure he could still work."

We do not have detailed information from current research on how patients negotiate the costs of care in other locations. Are they able to negotiate coverage by medical insurance companies? Is all medical travel financed by patients themselves or are some patients able to obtain government funding to cover the costs of medical procedures and/or travel? Inhorn (2015) calculates the cost of IVF and travel for treatment in Dubai at around $12,897 (USD) and acknowledged that many of the couples she interviewed (about one quarter of her sample) struggled to cover these expenses.

My research in Argentina painted a complex picture of patients' access to government funding and pointed to evident regional inequalities in relation to how decisions around funding were made, the amount of funding available and duration of the support (Vindrola-Padros, 2011). Obtaining the funding was a highly bureaucratic and burdensome process that, on some occasions, required that parents travel just to submit paperwork. Even if patients received some sort of support, it was never enough to cover all costs and families incurred great hardship while children obtained treatment away from home (Vindrola-Padros, 2011). Children knew this and commented on the impact of their treatment on family finances:

> **Adriana:** Sometimes I feel like stopping all of this.
> **Cecilia:** The treatment?
> **Adriana:** Yes, I mean, look at my family, we get 150 pesos from Plan Jefas [a government assistance program] and we have to spend all this money so that I can come here to get the treatment. I have two brothers and they have kids, my mom, and my dad and we are paying for the bus ticket for me, and the hotel. We put in the papers for a pension like eight months ago and haven't gotten anything.
> (Adriana, 16 years old)

Children undergoing oncology treatment in Argentina have access to a pension (a monthly government subsidy) when they are able to obtain a certificate of disability. Not all children diagnosed with cancer are eligible and it takes considerable work from the parents to obtain this certificate. This pension provides the family with access to PROFE (in English, Federal Program of Health and Medical Benefits). The PROFE is basically national medical coverage for the beneficiaries of the pension system (those who do not have any medical insurance), but the interviews with parents from different parts of the country indicated that it did not always guarantee access to free medical services. For instance, Camila's family in Salta (a northern province in Argentina) received good services from this program, obtaining full coverage of the costs for medication as well as the hotel where they stayed in Buenos Aires during treatment, the bus and plane tickets from Salta, and food expenses during travel and relocation. Sebastian's family from Entre Rios, in contrast, explained their negative experiences with PROFE as follows:

> "He has the pension and the PROFE, but the PROFE does not cover anything. You see it is the PROFE from the Province and I am in Concepcion del Uruguay and their central headquarter is in Parana and I can't go do the paperwork there. I am getting all of the medication from the hospital in Buenos Aires, but if I need anything else, I have to buy it myself and it doesn't cover everything […] I would have to change my residence to here [Buenos Aires] in order for it to cover me, but I live in Concepcion del Uruguay, so I can't change my residence."

I discussed the topic of the PROFE with a social worker who provided advice to parents on the paperwork they need to complete and the services they could apply for. She indicated that sometimes the PROFE acted as a double-edged sword:

> "The PROFE is experiencing a crisis and it is a cruel system. The problem that people have with this system is that the PROFE does not provide them with what they need. It doesn't cover medication and, in some cases, it doesn't cover travel expenses. Sometimes they go to the pharmacy to get medication and sometimes they have to go to 4 or 5 because they don't have it. They can't complain anywhere because the central is in La Plata [52 kilometers away from Buenos Aires]. The PROFE is sometimes worse than not having coverage, because if they had no assistance they could go to Desarrollo Social [Social Development Ministry, a government institution], but if they go having PROFE they tell them that they can't help them because they are already covered by PROFE."

The advice she gave to those families who could not get coverage from PROFE was to request it from the hospital or their council, but this certainly involved more bureaucratic processes. Some families also initiated lawsuits against PROFE, but these took a long time and the children had normally finished treatment by the time they were resolved. The issue of delays was also a common topic of discussion and five families who shared their stories with me had been waiting for their child's pension for over a year. Parents tried to deal with these delays by turning in the paperwork weeks before the deadlines, especially in terms of medication, but this strategy did not always work.

Families also tried to request government subsidies for transportation. In the case of long-distance travel, each province had funds to pay for families' bus or plane tickets, but the amount available and families' access to these funds varied by region. Law 2.596 in Argentina establishes a patient's right to use public transportation free of charge, but this might not always materialize in practice. Many families encountered problems when trying to obtain government funds to cover travel expenses. Ana's mother had a series of problems with the transportation passes as she could get free tickets from Corrientes (a northern province) to Buenos Aires, but could not get a return trip. At the time of the interview, she had severe economic difficulties because her province was not paying her hotel bill and she had to use the money she had saved to go home to pay these lodging expenses. Jessica's mom had no trouble getting bus tickets, but they denied her and her daughter the food services usually provided on long bus journeys. Emiliano and his mother had a similar problem with the food and were also denied the seating he required (with more leg space) due to his recent leg surgery. All of these parents complained with the respective authorities, but continued to face problems during long-distance travel.

Additional work needs to be done to uncover the real and hidden costs of medical travel. While some patients might travel seeking cheaper care, many others will incur great hardship to access services elsewhere. In addition to financial costs, medical travelers and their families must deal with the logistics of travel and the provision of care, booking medical appointments, obtaining access to medication and negotiating access to government pensions and other forms of support. These arrangements require a substantial amount of coordination and resources from the point of view of patients and their families and represent considerable emotional labor, a topic I will explore in greater detail in Chapter 7.

THE PROCESS OF TRAVELING

Even though there is recognition of the need to consider how movement transforms hospitals and healthcare itself (Whittaker & Chee, 2015), research on medical travel is limited in its exploration of the actual experiences of movement to access care. The act of traveling (both physical and in the imaginary) is a process imbued with meaning. Travel can be used in our search for something, as a rite of passage, as an escape, as a way to find a better life (Ateljevic & Doorne, 2000; Lanfrant, 1995; White & White, 2004). Travel experiences, both lived and told, have the potential to produce profound changes in the identities of travelers (Lean, 2014). The act of traveling, then, would reveal the nuances of this identity transformation and ways in which meanings surrounding disease and medical treatment might also be transformed in the process.

The quote that is included in the introductory chapter tries to allude to the complexity of medical travel experiences. The disruption to daily life posed by journeys, the exhaustion produced by the need to use multiple forms of transport, the stress generated by delays and unplanned events, all combine to produce particular experiences of medical travel. Ethnographic research has the potential to capture these layers of complexity, but, in the case of medical travel, has only glossed over them. The incorporation of a framework such as the critical (im)mobilities framework could help elucidate the practices and meanings of travel.

The mobilities literature has highlighted that "the body senses landscapes as it is moved through them" (Larsen et al., 2006). It explores the ontological nature of travel, as through movement, the essence of bodies or objects in motion is transformed (Appadurai, 1996). Travel is not a homogeneous practice, it involves different instances of movement and stasis, and the way in which movement is performed varies. While some patients travel for care in airplanes and are picked up at the airport in their destination country by representatives from a medical travel facilitation company, other patients travel by bus for days, across dirt roads, to access care. As Manderscheid (2009) has argued, "technologies of transportation and communication do not lead in a one-dimensional way to specific usage but their accessibility and appropriation is embedded in the emergence of practices which form specific socio-spatial arrangements."

While reading Manderscheid's (2009) work, I was reminded of a conversation I had with Camila, a 14-year-old girl from the northern province of Salta, who explained her most recent trip to Buenos Aires for treatment:

> "The other day, there was a strike and we had to leave on the 18th, so we had to leave at 11 p.m. on the 18th from my house. So there was a strike by the union [union of long-distance drivers], and we couldn't leave that day. We left the 19th at 9 a.m. We were supposed to reach Salta capital at 3 and my dad called the PROFE but they said the office would close by that time. They said they would get someone to go to the terminal so that we could get the papers, but the strike was close to Tartagal, so we had to stay until 3 and didn't reach Salta capital until 10 at night. The next day we had to be here [in Buenos Aires] because I had an appointment with my doctor. So we spent the night at the terminal because the offices weren't open at that time."

Camila had to sleep with her dad on a chair in a run-down bus terminal because they could not afford to stay in a hotel and the government office that normally pays for their lodging expenses (the PROFE) was closed by the time they got there. Camila recounted how they only had the food they brought with them from home to eat and how she had been so terribly cold that night, despite using her dad's coat as a blanket. Her narrative of travel brings to the surface so many different aspects of socio-economic inequalities in the country, the vulnerabilities of traveling families, their resilience, and national inequalities in the quality and distribution of transportation services.

Camila's story also points to the fact that the studies of medical travel that focus on the act of traveling itself could also make contributions to the mobilities literature as the travelers we study might have characteristics that are not common to all travelers. Medical travelers are not always in good health and might need assistance to travel. They might also need to travel with a carer (normally a close family member) and might also need the care of a medical professional as they travel. Their travel might be deemed more urgent and have to be arranged in specialized forms of transport (some of the patients I interviewed had to travel to Buenos Aires in air ambulances due to their delicate state and risk of contracting infections). What do these experiences of traveling while unwell tell us about the practices and meanings of travel more generally? While using a critical (im)mobilities framework, research on medical travel could help uncover trends in travel applicable to other health circumstances and travel contexts.

INTERACTIONS WITH MEDICAL FACILITIES AND PRACTITIONERS

As patients engage in medical travel and interact with destination medical facilities and practitioners, their experiences continue to diversify based on the local context and their own characteristics as patients (diagnosis, prognosis, health status) and individuals (class, gender, education, ethnicity, etc.). Even in the case of standardized medical pathways, medical treatment is not delivered in the same way to all patients. Perceptions of the skills of local healthcare practitioners intertwine with representations of 'deserving and undeserving patient populations' to create unique models of care. A critical (im)mobilities lens would attempt to explore the variability in the delivery of medical care to patients and identify any inequalities that might emerge in the process.

When examining the delivery of assisted reproductive technologies at a global scale, Gürtin has used the concept of "arenas of constraint" to comprehend the "different structural, ideological, and practical obstacles and applications serving to limit access, define prohibitions, and delineate parameters" for the application of treatments (2012, p. 83). Medical care, often perceived as a scarce resource, is negotiated in these arenas of constraint, producing different "incarnations" (Gürtin, 2012, p. 83) of care for each patient. Medical travel is often interpreted as the mechanism used to circumvent constraints and access care, yet ethnographic data has demonstrated that access to care during medical travel is seldom a straightforward process.

My work in Argentina (Vindrola-Padros, 2011), as well as Brage's (2018), has pointed to the barriers and complex negotiations children seeking care and their parents must undergo even after reaching their travel destination. Their narratives of treatment are filled with incessant struggles to obtain timely medical appointments, medication, funding, information, and high-quality care. Their journeys are lived as a constant process of bypassing gatekeepers, structural barriers, and fighting for their right to care.

Inhorn's (2015) research documents the plurality of journeys of reprotravelers (those using medical travel to access reproductive technologies) to global Dubai to access ARTs. Despite global trends in reproductive tourism, Inhorn argues that the delivery of IVF is shaped by local realities, "local theories of procreation, class hierarchies and accompanying stratifications in scientific literacy, gender relations and the varying embodiments of male and female infertility treatments, attitudes toward biomedicine and physician authority, and local theodicies and clerical decrees" (2015, p. 21). Her research follows couples through positive and negative experiences with doctors, instances of neglect and *malpraxis* as well as 'heroic' doctors who are able to deliver the 'miracle of life' (Inhorn, 2015).

Access to treatments and facilities is guided by evident infrastructural factors (like the ones we reviewed in Chapter 5), which could include policies and other forms of regulation of care, the physical availability of services in local facilities, and the capacity of patients to become a part of the flows of those seeking care. Healthcare professionals form part of this infrastructure and play an active role in promoting and hindering medical travel, yet I decided to discuss their role in medical travel in this chapter as I felt it was important to explore how they shape medical travel experiences.

Gürtin (2012) refers to healthcare professionals and other types of staff members (she uses the term practitioners), as "interface agents." The concept of interface agent is used to allude to practitioners' role in "transforming universal scientific knowledge about assisted reproduction into culturally expedient applications for their patients" (Gürtin, 2012, p. 81). Their role as interface agents includes translation, mediation, and representation of ideas about care in general, medicine, clinical evidence, specific medical treatments, and patient groups, creating localized and unique ways of delivering services (Gürtin, 2012).

According to Gürtin (2012), their role as interface agents also involves making decisions about protocols and patient pathways, ultimately defining who travels, when, how, and where. An in-depth exploration of their role in care delivery allows us to visualize the ways in which the individual actions and decisions made by practitioners shape the wider infrastructures that facilitate or inhibit patients' movements and their ultimate access to treatment (Gürtin, 2012). These decisions or actions can be those directly impacting patients' capacity to access a particular treatment at home (i.e. the design of regulation to make access to certain treatments illegal), but they do not necessarily have to be of this magnitude.

Ethnographic research, with its focus on daily and micro-level interactions, has pointed to more nuanced ways in which practitioners might shape patients' and carers' experiences of travel and care. In my research in Argentina, the shaping of patients' experiences was as direct as a referral to a hospital far away from the patients' place of origin (meaning that patients would probably need to travel), or as subtle as the rolling of the practitioner's eyes to indicate that the care in the local hospital would not be the best option for the child's care. Neglect and bad communication between patients, parents, and practitioners could also entice patients and their families to seek care elsewhere.

Medical travel research points to mainly positive representations of practitioners in destination hospitals. These practitioners were often represented as "doctors who care" (Speier, 2016, p. 84), who spend plenty of time with patients and are not driven by financial gain, but the desire to genuinely help their patients (Dalstrom, 2013; Inhorn, 2015; Speier, 2016). As interface agents, then, doctors and other hospital staff members shape perceptions and experiences of care in destination hospitals, in several cases, making these better adapted to patients' needs.

An area that has received little attention in the medical travel literature is that of follow-up care and the potential connections between practitioners in the place of origin and those in the medical travel destination. It makes me wonder, what happens when the patient goes home after the procedure?

What happens if they require follow-up care at home? How do these interface agents operate in these circumstances? What happens and who takes over responsibility for care if there are any complications? Due to the designs of most of the studies on medical travel (most located in medical travel destinations) and the nature of the procedures that were studied (one-off elective procedures), our knowledge of medical travel destinations ends when medical travelers leave the destination hospital. Research is rarely carried out with patients in their place of origin after receiving treatment or a procedure elsewhere.

A few studies have captured the back and forth travels of patients and describe some aspects of returning home after treatment through the patients' and families' narratives of treatment. Inhorn (2015), for instance, presented rich details on the lives of couples who traveled to Dubai on several occasions to conceive a child, and Speier (2016) presented similar scenarios for couples traveling to the Czech Republic. However, the interactions (if any) of care delivery systems at home and medical travel destinations seem to be unexplored.

Both Brage (2018) and I (Vindrola-Padros, 2011) tried to get a glimpse of the care delivered to patients when they went back home. Brage's (2018) ethnography plays an important role in examining the shared care processes in Argentina, as she seeks to describe how telemedicine is currently used by one of the pediatric cancer specialist centers in Buenos Aires to deliver care to children in the north-east and north-west regions of the country after they go home, preventing them from traveling to Buenos Aires again.

In my ethnography, I was able to follow the journeys of children who had relapsed (that is, their cancer had come back) after their treatment had been completed in Buenos Aires. In one of the cases, the relapse was caught in the place of origin (the others were identified in Buenos Aires during follow-up consultations that families traveled for), but the family's inability to pay for the expenses of traveling back to Buenos Aires to undergo new treatment severely affected the child's chances of survival. When Diego (7 years old) talked about this issue he said, "my mom was working and we couldn't pay for the bus ticket and now it's back."

Adherence to treatment is not usually a concern in Argentina as biomedical concordance is high. However, there are evident economic factors that can prevent families from following up with medical consultation after treatment such as the suspension of government funding, employment restrictions, or the payment of loans obtained to cover the expenses of the child's initial treatment. Diego's mom described the situation as follows: "after a while, I could not get the money to come back [to Buenos Aires, about 800 kilometers from their place of origin]. When I was able to find work again, I would put some money aside, I would save and save until I had enough to come back." In cases of relapse, the timing of treatment is an important indicator of the patient's prognosis (Guarneri et al., 2011). Stories like Diego's provide a window into the mechanics of the political economy of health, where those who cannot afford to pay for the bus trip back to Buenos Aires will not have the same chance of survival as those who can.

CONCLUSIONS

In this chapter, I have sought to explore the diversity of medical travel experiences by outlining how these vary throughout the different stages of treatment and travel (deciding to travel in the face of a diagnosis, arranging the logistics of travel, interacting with medical facilities and practitioners, and returning home). A critical (im)mobilities framework, with its emphasis on differential mobility empowerments, allows us to examine the reasons why not all who desire to move will be able to do so. It will also shed light on the diversity of these journeys. The ability to move and the resources required to achieve movement are negotiated on a daily basis with interface agents and through arenas of constraint, creating particular experiences of travel and care. In the next chapter, I will explore the role of emotions in these processes of negotiation.

CHAPTER SEVEN
Affective journeys and the imagination

An important contribution of the mobilities turn was the recognition of the ways in which emotions, feelings, and the imagination permeate experiences of travel (Sherry & Urry, 2006). Many times, movement is sought to fuel particular emotional responses; the thrill, excitement, and feeling of adventure that leads many to travel to unknown places. When a new place shows promise of a better life or a cure, travel embodies a sense of hope.

A critical (im)mobilities framework would seek to recognize these symbolic dimensions of travel, but understand them in the context of prevailing social, political, and economic inequalities. It would explore how emotional responses are shaped by histories of exclusion, discrimination, or frustration. A critical perspective would uncover how feelings of hope might only be triggered in those who see a potential capacity to travel, but would not be available to all. This chapter grapples with the emotional aspects of medical travel, discussing the research carried out to date on this topic and bringing in examples from my own research to highlight how experiences of medical travel are shaped by how we think and feel.

DREAMS AND IMAGINED FUTURES

As we saw in Chapter 6, decisions to seek medical services elsewhere are made in relation to ideas about local care, potential care available elsewhere and perceptions of our right or possibility to access this care. We have already discussed the role the imagination plays in decisions to travel for services and the selection of medical travel destinations. In this chapter, I would like to explore other ways in which the imagination shapes experiences of medical travel.

In their exploration of couples' experiences of reproductive travel, both Speier (2016) and Inhorn (2015) discuss the ways in which imagined notions of parenthood and family life motivate couples to seek assisted reproductive technologies, sometimes at the expense of their finances, time, and bodies. Whittaker and Speier have argued that travel for ARTs are not a "one-off" procedure, "but rather a commitment to a range of tests and procedures across the course of a 'cycle'" (2010, p. 367). The desire to fulfill their own and social expectations of parenthood leads many couples to maintain a strong commitment to these tests and procedures, often undergoing a series of cycles in one or more locations (Speier, 2016). They 'get through' these difficult times by picturing the ultimate goal of their travels: coming back home with a baby.

Representations of beauty and femininity also instigate medical travel, as in the ethnography developed by Aizura (2010) on gender reassignment surgery in Thailand. Aizura (2010) describes how materials used to advertise "sex change surgery" appeal to imagined notions of womanhood as "soft" and "delicate." For medical travelers, the process of GRS not only involves assimilating these notions of womanhood, but specifically engaging with symbolic representations of Thai femininity through a series of rituals used to mark the liminality of their position (Aizura, 2010).

Inhorn (2011) uses the term "diasporic dreaming" when she analyzes the experiences of Middle Eastern couples who dream of making test-tube babies in their country of origin. This decision to participate in return medical travel is influenced by 'push' factors (i.e. cultural discrimination in the current place of residence) and cultural, moral, and psychological 'pull' factors (Inhorn, 2011, p. 587). These 'pull' factors are fueled by what Inhorn has described as "both patriotic and nostalgic attachments to home," where medical services back home are seen as of superior quality to those in the place of residence (Inhorn, 2011).

As discussed in Chapter 6, the imagination plays a central role in the shaping of decisions to participate in medical travel; feelings, emotions, and different forms of attachments combine to ensemble particular travel and care imaginaries. These imaginaries might materialize in actual experiences of travel, but can also remain as imagined, potential journeys. Inhorn (2011) reflects on the fact that many of the couples who shared their stories with her had 'unrealistic' dreams of going back home as they could never go back due to economic and political constraints on their capacity to move freely (i.e. refugee status or discrimination faced by Middle Easterners post 9/11) or the violence experienced in their countries.

Perhaps these dreams would remain suspended, somewhat immobile even, in their memories until they were transformed into another dream of a more realistic form of medical travel or shattered completely when medical travel could not even be considered an option. A critical (im)mobilities framework could help us explore these instances of imaginaries that appear to be suspended in time. As mentioned in Chapter 5, studies of medical travel could benefit from a more in-depth exploration of the immobile. The immobile could be explored in the imagination, focusing on those ideas, memories, dreams, and desires that remain fixed, 'stuck' or suspended in time. These idealized notions of both travel and care could be studied by themselves or in connection with actual experiences of medical travel, if these are ever performed.

HOME AWAY FROM HOME

In his ethnography of German patients seeking reproductive services in Spain and the Czech Republic, Bergmann (2011a, 2011b) argued that when transnational assisted reproduction has been studied quantitatively or using rational choice models, it has relied on the role of push and pull factors in patient decision-making and neglected the power of emotions and the imagination. In the experiences of medical travel he analyzed, he was able to see the instrumental role that patients' desire to "feel at home" played in their selection of medical travel destinations (Bergmann, 2011b, p. 605). Feeling at home entailed less medicalized atmospheres and doctors with whom they felt they could communicate well (i.e. who spoke German or English) (Bergmann, 2011b).

The search for services in facilities where patients "feel at home" has been mentioned frequently across many studies. Whittaker and Chee (2015) described the creation of hybrid hospitals, which combined hospital spaces with more hotel-like environments designed to make patients comfortable. Speier (2016) highlighted how couples chose clinics that seemed well organized, clean and where staff were able to communicate in a number of different languages. Conceive, the clinic where Inhorn (2015) carried out her ethnography of reproductive medical travel to Dubai, also shared these characteristics, with all staff members speaking English as well as other commonly spoken languages in the region. Ackerman's (2010) study of medical travel for cosmetic surgery in Costa Rica delved into the infrastructures developed to care for traveling patients and ensure they were relaxed and "feeling at home."

While considerable efforts are made to ensure medical travelers are comfortable during their procedures and recovery, some studies describe instances where patient experience lacks the warm feelings of being at home. Both Brage (2018) and I (Vindrola-Padros, 2011) describe instances of frustration with care, nostalgia and homesickness. Rodrigo's mom explained her son's last hospitalization in Buenos Aires as follows:

> "Let me tell you what happened to us the last time Rodrigo was hospitalized. We were next to a child with fever. I wondered, the child has fever and he is next to my child […] They then moved him [Rodrigo] to another room, next to an adolescent girl who had a headache. But then you start to think because you are moving the child through a shared hallway and the bathroom is shared with other patients, and the utensils are shared and the chamber pot is shared. And you are always tense because of this, the building is old and you go get the chamber pot at 3 am and you have roaches walking around there […] You have to bring your own supplies if you can afford them or if you can remember to do so."

The nature of the treatment sought in Buenos Aires meant that the families both Brage (2018) and I (Vindrola-Padros, 2011) worked with had to remain away from home for months, many times not being able to go home for a short visit during the entire duration of treatment (this represented years in the case of some families). This meant many parents needed to get used to living in a new, and sometimes frightening, city. Martin's mom explained how she felt before arriving to Buenos Aires:

> "For many mothers that don't know the movement here and they get scared, like it happened to me when they told me 'you have to go to Buenos Aires.' I said well where am I going to go? What am I going to do? It is scary when they tell you I am referring you to Buenos Aires for this reason. It is scary because it is a big place, and maybe you don't know how to get around. You are used to something small that you can handle, that you can walk from one place to another […] When they told me that they were referring me to Buenos

Aires, my whole world came tumbling down because I didn't know what I would do here, I didn't know anything."

She eventually got to know the bus routes in her area and could move around the city with ease, but not all parents engaged well with their new surroundings. Rodrigo's mom said, "I talked to several [parents] who were staying in pensions [low-cost hotels] that don't go out. They stay locked in. Buenos Aires scares them, they don't know how to get around, they are scared. They don't know anyone, have no friends, they are alone. I think loneliness is probably the worst thing."

Medical travelers seek to obtain care in a place that feels like home away from home. While some destinations are able to provide this type of service, not all patients receive care in these types of facilities. A critical (im)mobilities framework with its focus on differing degrees of power and privilege can help uncover the factors that lead to varying types of care.

AFFECTIVE LABOR AND CARING FOR MEDICAL TRAVELERS

Several studies have documented the different types of labor involved in caring for medical travelers. In their work on reproductive medical travel, Whittaker and Speier argue that medical travel facilitation companies insert a "discourse of affective labor, care and nurturing within a reproductive experience that is otherwise devoid of all familiar relationships" (2010, p. 372). This affective labor helps put patients at ease in what would otherwise be cold commercial relationships.

In her study of the experiences of North American patients who travel to the Czech Republic to access reproductive services, Speier (2016) argues that the medical travel industry needs to be framed as global care routes tangled in intimate labor. She draws from Boris and Parrenas' (2010) work on intimate labor, which defines it as "work that entails bodily and emotional closeness as well as intimate knowledge of personal information" (Speier, 2016, p. 45). By focusing on IVF brokers, Speier (2016) explores how these actors assume a caring responsibility over medical travelers and their companions, which requires congenial and empathetic personalities, and the sharing of personal intimacies to create open and trusting relationships. Through this caring role, brokers provide solace and comfort to anxious and worried patients (Speier, 2011). Ackerman also explores the affective carework involved in the "business of transforming and tending North Americans' bodies" (2010, p. 406) after undergoing cosmetic surgery in Costa Rica. This affective carework is delivered in a context where surgery is not obtained in the quest for beauty, but is sought as a result of a larger project of restoring mental health, ensuring transitions or enabling a rebirth (Ackerman, 2010).

Affective labor is not only performed by those who deliver services to traveling patients, but also by the family members who travel with them. Family members are seen as responsible for prolonging their life or improving its quality. In Kangas' (2007) ethnographic account of Yemeni patients' experiences of international medical travel, she highlights situations where financially abled households who did not send ill family members for medical treatment abroad were criticized. She argues, "should a patient die abroad, the family could reassure themselves, and others, that they had held nothing back" (Kangas, 2007, p. 299).

Intertwined with medical travel, then, are notions of family duties, loyalty, and dedication. This deep sense of responsibility surfaced in many of the interviews I carried out in Argentina with the parents of ill children who had traveled long distances to find a 'cure' for their child. "If I have to take him to China, I don't know how I will do it, but I will take him to China. Wherever he can have the best quality of life," said Claudio's mom while we waited together for a bus to the hospital. The phrase "from here to China" was frequently used to express the long distances parents were willing to travel to save their child's life. Marta's mom explained how the needs of the child prevailed over hers and all of the other members of the family:

> "What I wanted was a place where she would be fine. I wanted her well-being, I wasn't worried about me, my well-being. I wanted her to be well, to start treatment, to not waste more time [...] I don't even care about eating or anything, I have to be well for her [...] Today you have to leave many things behind, but it is for their own good. I didn't even think about it. I didn't doubt it."

Parents' search for a cure did not stop when biomedical treatments 'failed to work,' as many families who were told by doctors that nothing else could be done continued to search for other types of care. As mentioned earlier in the book, Rodrigo's family visited a 'healing priest' to see if he could improve Rodrigo's health condition. Parkin's (2014) research in the eastern region of East Africa touches on a similar point regarding travel for non-biomedical treatment. According to him, in the Kenyan coastal area, biomedicine is recognized as suitable only for addressing acute symptoms, while chronic conditions require non-biomedical healers who are capable of delivering more holistic care (Parkin, 2014). An interesting finding is that this travel to non-biomedical healers is seen as a healing process in itself, as the sacrifice of the journey and the visits made to kin while searching for treatment are thought to contribute to the patient's well-being (Parkin, 2014). In this sense, Parkin (2014) argues that it is appropriate to consider medical travel journeys as a form of pilgrimage as the travel needs to fulfill therapeutic-spiritual satisfaction (see also Song, 2010).

Accompanying family members are there to ensure the patient's needs are met at all times. When this is not the case, it is their duty "to fight" for the patient. One of the mothers who shared her story with me in Buenos Aires reflected on the case of another child receiving treatment in the same hospital as her son: "I remember the parents of this girl who were in a dirty place, a dirty hotel. You see, the child has to be in a certain place. There are parents who realize this and others who don't. Those who realize it have a hard time. The parents of this girl complained and they changed their room, but you have to fight so that they give you an appropriate place for your child." Camila's dad described a similar situation:

> "Sometimes our trip becomes very difficult because our journey is long. I have to think about things, because sometimes you have to sign all of these papers. Sometimes we miss the appointment times and we have to get new ones. You have to do a lot of things. Sometimes they cut the bus route and you miss the appointment and you have to stay for a month before you can get a new one. You have to fight a lot, go to offices, go to Social Services."

This process of fighting takes an emotional toll on parents, who confess feeling "burned out," "exhausted," and "nearing desperation." "It is hard," Lucia's mom explained, "you have to be a special person because I see how many parents get depressed, they get really bad. That does not help the treatment. You have to find strength where you thought you didn't have any, because you have no other choice." This carer role is not only about facilitating bureaucratic processes or ensuring the patient arrives to medical appointments on time. In some cases, it also entails becoming somewhat of a medical expert to demand care is delivered appropriately. While carrying out my fieldwork, one mother became upset as she shared an experience she had gone through earlier that week, "the other day, the nurses did something wrong because they could not find his notes. I keep a copy of everything, but they didn't wait for me. He needs to be hospitalized for a few more days so they can sort it out."

Parents kept track of the child's treatment by keeping notebooks with detailed notes on the treatment the child received, any symptoms and test results. Sebastian's mom had impressive record-keeping skills and kept a folder with photocopies of each analysis, medical test and procedure, with dates, times, and names of physicians as well as photographs of the child at each stage. The parents indicated how sometimes these notebooks were requested by the healthcare professionals and how they would check the mother's notes (in addition to or instead of their own medical records) before administering drugs to the child. Martin's mom described the information she wrote in her notebook as follows:

> "I would write down the water he would drink, how many times he went to the bathroom. I would weigh what he did in the bathroom and check that there were no red threads of blood produced by the diarrhea. I would check that what he did was normal, that he did not have a red butt. From the moment you get up to the moment you go to sleep, you are aware of what they are doing 24 hours a day."

CONCLUSIONS

Experiences of medical travel are shaped by ideas of care, travel, daily life, and dreams of life as a result of medical travel. Journeys are enacted to reach a "higher purpose" (dreams of motherhood or a cure) and become imbued with deep cultural meaning, sometimes representing a form of pilgrimage. These journeys require a deep emotional investment on behalf of the patients and those who care for them and a considerable amount of labor (both physical and emotional) is required to ensure patients' needs are met.

A critical (im)mobilities framework would seek to explore the role emotions play across individuals, shaping experiences of travel in different ways. It would also highlight how hope, loyalty, love, and dedication can empower patients and their families to seek care elsewhere despite evident barriers. The analysis of emotions, the imagination and other symbolic dimensions of medical travel needs to be done in relation to an appreciation of infrastructures and exploration of the practices of medical travel. In the next chapter, I explore how these dimensions can be combined to study medical travel as a complex phenomenon and highlight future areas of exploration.

CHAPTER EIGHT
Future directions in medical travel research

> *"In a splintered world, we must address the splinters."*
> (Geertz, 2000, p. 221)

The quote above by Clifford Geertz is used in his essay "The World in Pieces" to shed light on the inequalities that permeate every aspect of our lives. He made a call to abandon totalizing concepts such as tradition, nation, culture, ideology, and state, and, instead, consider the plurality of ways of being and belonging, the particularities of everyday life (Geertz, 2000). In this chapter, I will discuss how medical travel research can respond to this call by uncovering the granularities of human experiences and thoughts of mobility.

Considerable progress has been made in the analysis of people's perceptions and experiences of medical travel and the ways in which these are shaped by local realities (Kangas, 2007; Sobo et al., 2009). Authors have highlighted the cultural desires and care preferences of traveling patients, as well as the cultural appeals made by medical travel promoters and healthcare facilities (Sobo et al., 2011; Sobo, 2015). However, gaps remain in our understanding of the political economies of healthcare and medical travel, and, in particular, the relationship between inequalities in the distribution of medical services and medical travel.

The application of critical frameworks to the study of medical travel can allow us to see medical travel as a consequence of the unequal distribution of medical services, as well as a producer of inequalities. When we "ride along," "walk with," and immerse ourselves in the daily lives of medical travelers and those who care for them, we are able to examine movement across multiple locales and scales, in time, practice, and in the imagination (Dalakoglou & Harvey, 2012). We can theorize mobility as a complex social process, entailing different modalities and layers of movement (Chalfin, 2016), and access to healthcare can be critically examined to uncover relations of power and structural inequalities that guarantee high-quality services for some and deny them for others (Willen et al., 2011).

OVERVIEW OF THE THEORETICAL AND METHODOLOGICAL APPROACHES IN THE BOOK

Before presenting a future agenda for research, I felt it would be appropriate to give a brief overview of the work carried out in this book to inform future studies on this topic. The aim of this book was to present an overview of the critical perspectives used to understand processes of medical travel and demonstrate how one critical approach, the critical (im)mobilities framework, can be used to bring the analysis of inequalities to the forefront of studies of medical travel. The critical (im)mobilities framework stemmed from a wider 'mobilities turn' in the social sciences that sought to study mobilities in their own centrality and singularity (D'Andrea et al., 2011; Urry, 2007). This framework was developed to account for the role of asymmetries in power in the shaping of episodes of movement and stasis (Soderström et al., 2013), identifying the structures that allowed some to move, while preventing others from doing so, as well as how factors such as class, gender, and ethnicity contributed to the creation of particular types of movement, and perceptions and experiences of staying still.

In this book, I used the critical (im)mobilities framework as the lens through which to analyze existing literature on medical travel. I found three main dimensions from this framework particularly helpful for the field of medical travel:

1. ***Infrastructures***: The examination of infrastructures, or the roads, objects, networks, and institutions that can both facilitate and constrain movement (Korpela, 2016; Urry, 2007) to explore the wide range of actors involved in the creation and maintenance of medical travel processes.
2. ***Differential mobility empowerments***: The recognition of the highly differentiated nature of medical travel (Adey, 2006; Cresswell, 2011) and the (re)production of these differences by the performance of movement in social worlds that are shaped by politics, history, economics, and cultures.

3. *Affective (im)mobilities*: The acknowledgment of the ways in which emotions, feelings, and the imagination permeate experiences of care and travel (Sherry & Urry, 2006) and examination of these in the context of prevailing social, political, and economic inequalities (Salazar, 2011).

AREAS OF STRENGTH IN MEDICAL TRAVEL RESEARCH

It is important to consider the wide range of geographical contexts and medical procedures that have been studied so far. Many of these texts have already engaged with critical theoretical frameworks, considering concepts such as stratified care or arenas of constraint, which seek to stress inequalities present in both travel and care delivery and access. Several authors have explored the factors that play a role in decisions to engage in medical travel and the factors considered when selecting medical travel destinations (Ackerman, 2010; Aizura, 2010; Bergmann, 2011a, 2011b; Edmonds, 2011; Green, 2016; Inhorn, 1996, 2003, 2007, 2008, 2015; Nolan & Schneider, 2011; Sobo et al., 2011; Song, 2010; Speier, 2011, 2016; Whittaker, 2008).

Another area explained in detail has been the role of intermediaries, in the form of medical travel facilitation companies (through websites or face-to-face interviews) or other types of brokers, in the development and maintenance of patient flows (Ackerman, 2010; Bergmann, 2011a, 2011b; Dalstrom, 2013; Sobo et al., 2011; Speier, 2011, 2016). Considerable amount of work has also explored patients' perceptions of the place where care is obtained and the quality of the care delivered by healthcare professionals (Brage, 2018; Gürtin, 2012; Inhorn, 2015; Speier, 2016; Vindrola-Padros, 2011, 2012; Whittaker & Chee, 2015). The effects of medical travel on medical facilities, staff, and local populations in destination countries has also been explored (Ormond, 2013, 2015a, 2015b; Chen & Flood, 2013). Finally, some research has focused on the financial implications and emotional burden of seeking care far from home (Brage, 2018; Kangas, 2007, 2010; Vindrola-Padros, 2011, 2012).

FUTURE AREAS OF EXPLORATION

In addition to identifying the contributions of existing research in the field of medical travel, the application of a critical (im)mobilities framework to existing work has pointed to areas that have been neglected and would, therefore, benefit from further exploration. These areas include:

FAILED ATTEMPTS AT MEDICAL TRAVEL OR IMAGINED JOURNEYS THAT NEVER MATERIALIZE

When examining the role of infrastructures as motivating and hindering movement, a question that emerged concerned the cases where infrastructures play a deterring role in processes of medical travel. What happens when patients consider seeking treatment elsewhere, but cannot engage in medical travel? What are the factors preventing them from doing so? How are these journeys imagined and how long do they remain in the imagination? Do these imagined journeys change through time and do they shape experiences of accessing local care?

The concept of immobility, with its focus on episodes of transition, waiting, emptiness, "stuckness," and fixity (Khan, 2016) can be useful when exploring these experiences of failed or never-tried attempts of medical travel. This concept can also be used to explore imagined journeys, their relative immutability and destruction when dreams of travel are abandoned. These immobilities cannot be understood in isolation from their historical roots, the politics, cultures, and economic processes that shape them (see Vindrola-Padros et al., forthcoming). (Im)mobilities are sociocultural constructs; they have meaning and value (Salazar, 2010a). We can detail how mobility is embedded in cultural discourses, manifested in imaginaries, and (re)configured in everyday life (Salazar & Smart, 2011). The detail of the everyday, obtained by an immersion in the context of research, can be used as a window into the particularities of the locale, but also as a connection to other relevant scales. Through the analysis of the local, we are able to capture processes leading to immobility that are operating at other, more abstract, and perhaps more global levels (Tsing, 2005).

THE LOGISTICS OF MEDICAL TRAVEL

A limited amount of research has engaged with the arrangements that need to be put in place by traveling patients and their families to seek care elsewhere. The few studies that provided this level of detail indicated that medical travel is a highly burdensome process, entailing great physical and emotional labor (Brage, 2018; Kangas, 2007, 2010; Vindrola-Padros, 2011, 2012). Additional work needs to be carried out to understand the financial implications of medical travel and how these expenses are normally covered. Other types of arrangements back home (i.e. employment, childcare, housework) as well as in the medical travel destination (i.e. accommodation, paperwork, other services), need to be explored. Movements, ideas of travel and enacted journeys are dependent on the characteristics of the individuals involved, the place of origin, the real or imagined destination, the mode of transport, the time of travel, etc. In order to grasp the complexities of these scales and networks (through which people, things, and ideas move), we need dynamic epistemological approximations and sensibilities (Salazar, 2010b; Salazar & Smart, 2011). This detailed description of the more micro-level processes that facilitate medical travel could benefit greatly from a critical (im)mobilities framework, as this lens could be used to explore how contextual factors and social and economic inequalities influence the types of arrangements patients and their families are able to make.

INTERNAL MEDICAL TRAVEL

An important aim of this book has been the consideration of multiple forms of medical travel, not just international travel. An argument was made early on in the book, which stated that all types of travel entailed material and symbolic processes that needed to be taken into consideration in patients' quest for care. Internal and more localized forms of travel also have meaning and represent challenges for patients and families. Their study could make important contributions to our examination of international medical travel, as experiences of patients having to cross national borders could be compared with those who move within their regions (potentially crossing other types of borders). Can we identify similar instances of care inequalities? What are the strategies patients and families use to negotiate barriers to care when travel requires global displacement vs. when travel is more localized, though not necessarily shorter or easier?

THE EXPERIENCES OF THOSE ACCOMPANYING MEDICAL TRAVELERS

A surprising finding was the lack of research on the experiences of those accompanying medical travelers. Some of the research on reproductive tourism engaged with the views of partners who traveled with the patient (Inhorn, 2015; Speier, 2016), but on several occasions partners were also receiving some form of intervention or diagnostic procedure. The ethnographies on travel for pediatric oncology treatment (Brage, 2018; Vindrola-Padros, 2011, 2012), Kangas' work (2007, 2010) and Crooks' studies of caregivers (Crooks et al., 2017) are probably the main texts to show the role played by accompanying family members. Future ethnographies of medical travel would benefit from exploring the role of these companions, as they negotiate care for patients, expand their sense of loyalty and dedication beyond borders, and experience movement with the patient to potentially unknown destinations (see Vindrola-Padros, forthcoming).

EPISTEMOLOGICAL OPENNESS AND INVIGORATION

Regardless of the areas of exploration outlined above, an important contribution to the study of medical travel will be the development of conceptual openness and creativity. According to Dalakoglou and Harvey (2012), when we are able to locate material and social relations without needing to decide in advance on the ontology, the scale or the extension of such relationships, we open ourselves to the possibility of being surprised, of encountering the unexpected. Rivoal and Salazar (2013) have highlighted the contributions of serendipity, or "the art of making an unsought finding" (Van Andel, 1994, p. 631). This requires approaching the field of study with a critical reflection of one's own preconceptions and undergoing a continuous exercise of self-reflection to ensure openness to ways of thinking and behaving that might not have been expected. As Olivier de Sardan has argued, we need "to observe what [we] are not prepared to see" (1995, p. 77).

This capacity to engage with serendipity in such a productive manner will make our research capable of invigorating the fields of mobility studies and medical travel with new areas of research, theories, and methodologies. Openness will mean seeing new aspects of (im)mobilities, reframing them or turning them on their head. It will mean questioning categories that are taken for granted, decentering our analysis, acknowledging our own locality and mobility and the locality and mobility of the topics, people, and things we study (Österlund-Pötzsch, 2017).

CONCLUSIONS

As more and more people travel to obtain care far from home, a critical analysis of medical travel becomes even more relevant. Who travels, why they decide to travel, how travel is performed, when travel is carried out, and the medical travel destination are all dimensions shaped by prevalent inequalities in our society. From a critical perspective, medical travel is not just the result of consumer choice to seek better and more affordable care, it is also the manifestation of the unequal distribution of medical services and the categorization of some patients as deserving and others as undeserving of adequate care.

This book proposed the use of the critical (im)mobilities framework to explore the infrastructures that allow or hinder movement, the use of mobility as capital and its unequal distribution, and the role of emotions in the creation of journeys, both real and imagined. We have embarked on a complex journey through studies of medical travel that has taken us from couples' experiences of reproductive tourism in the Czech Republic to parents' search for pediatric oncology treatment in Argentina. I have only explored three potential dimensions of the critical (im)mobilities framework. It is time for us to be bold and creative as we move into the areas of medical travel that remain unexplored.

BIBLIOGRAPHY

Abriata, M. G., & Moreno F. (2010). Cancer en la población de menores de 15 años en Argentina. *Revista Argentina de Salud Publica*, 1(3), 42–45.

Ackerman, S. (2010). Plastic paradise: Transforming bodies and selves in Costa Rica's cosmetic surgery tourism industry. *Medical Anthropology*, 29(4), 403–423.

Adey, P. (2006). If mobility is everything then it is nothing: Towards a relational politics of (im)mobilities. *Mobilities*, 1(1), 75–94.

Adey, P., & Bissell, D. (2010). Mobilities, meetings, and futures: An interview with John Urry. *Environment and Planning D: Society and Space*, 28(1), 1–16.

Agamben, G. (1998). *Homo sacer: Sovereign power and bare life*. Stanford, CA: Stanford University Press.

Agamben, G. (2005). *State of exception*. Chicago, IL: University of Chicago Press.

Agee, B., Funkhouser, E., Roseman, J., Fawal, H., Holmberg, S., & Vermund, S. (2006). Migration patterns following HIV diagnosis among adults residing in the nonurban Deep South. *AIDS Care*, 18(1), S51–S58.

Aizura, A. (2010). Feminine transformations: Gender reassignment surgical tourism in Thailand. *Medical Anthropology*, 29(4), 424–443.

Alsharif, M. J., Labonte, R., & Lu, Z. (2010). Patients beyond borders: A study of medical tourists in four countries. *Global Social Policy*, 10, 315–335.

Andrews, M. (2004). Vacation makeovers. *US News and World Report*, 19 January.

Appadurai, A. (1996). *Modernity at large: Cultural dimensions of globalization*. Minneapolis, MN: University of Minnesota Press.

Appadurai, A. (2003). Sovereignty without territoriality: Notes for a postnational geography. In S. Low & D. Lawrence-Zuniga (eds.), *The anthropology of space and culture: Locating culture* (pp. 337-349). Malden, MA: Blackwell Publishing.

Armstrong, D. (1988). Space and time in British general practice. In M. Lock & D. Gordon (eds.), *Biomedicine examined* (pp. 207-225). Dordrecht: Kluwer Academic Publishers.

Armus, D. (2007). *La ciudad impura: Salud, tuberculosis y cultura en Buenos Aires, 1870-1950*. Buenos Aires: Edhasa.

Arora, R. S., Eden T., & Pizer B. (2007). The problem of treatment abandonment in children from developing countries with cancer. *Pediatric Blood Cancer*, 49, 941-946.

Arunanondchai, J., & Carsten, F. (2007). Trade in health services in the ASEAN region. *Health Promotion International*, 21(S1), 59-66.

Ateljevic, I., & Doorne, S. (2000). Tourism as an escape: Long-term travelers in New Zealand. *Tourism Analysis*, 5(2-4), 131-136.

Baer, H., Singer, S., & Johnson J. (1986). Toward a Critical Medical Anthropology. *Social Science and Medicine*, 23(2), 95-98.

Baer, H., Singer, M., & Susser, I. (2003). *Medical anthropology and the world system*. Westport, CN: Praeger.

Bærenholdt, J. (2013). Governmobility: The powers of mobility. *Mobilities*, 8(1), 20-34.

Belmartino, S. (2005). Estado social o estado de compromiso? Agotamiento, crisis y reformulación de las instituciones de atención médica. Argentina 1920-1945. In D. Lvovich, & J. Suriano (eds.), *Las Políticas Sociales en Perspectiva Histórica: Argentina, 1870-1952* (pp. 111-134). Buenos Aires: Universidad Nacional de General Sarmiento and Prometeo Libros.

Belmartino, S., & Bloch, C. (1982). Politicas estatales y seguridad social en Argentina. *Cuadernos Medico Sociales*, 22, 1-16.

Bello, M., & Becerril-Montekio, V. (2011). Sistema de salud de Argentina. *Salud Publica de Mexico*, 53(2), S96-S108.

Bendixen, S., & Eriksen, T. H. (2018). Time and the other: Waiting and hope among irregular migrants. In M. K. Janeja & A. Bandak (eds.), *Ethnographies of waiting* (pp. 87-112). London/New York: Bloomsbury.

Bennett, B. (2000). Reproductive technology, public policy and single motherhood. *Sydney Law Review*, 22, 625–635.

Bergmann, S. (2011a). Fertility tourism: Circumventive routes that enable access to reproductive technologies and substances. *Signs*, 36(2), 280–289.

Bergmann, S. (2011b). Reproductive agency and projects: Germans searching for egg donation in Spain and the Czech Republic. *Reproductive BioMedicine Online*, 23(5), 600–608.

Bidart Campos, G. (1989). Argentina. In H. Fuenzalida-Puelma, & S. Scholle Connor (eds.), *El derecho a la salud en las Américas. Estudio constitucional comparado* (pp. 25–43). Washington, D.C.: PAHO.

Biehl, J. (2005). *Vita: Life in a zone of social abandonment*. Berkeley, CA: University of California Press.

Bissell, D., & Fuller, G. (2001). *Stillness in a mobile world*. London: Routledge.

Boellstorff, T., & Lindquist, J. (2004). Bodies of emotion: Rethinking culture and emotion through Southeast Asia. *Ethnos*, 69(4), 437–444.

Bookman, M., & Bookman, K. (2007). *Medical tourism in developing countries*. New York: Palgrave MacMillan.

Boris, E., & Salazar Parrenas, R., (eds.) (2010). *Intimate labors: Cultures, technologies and politics of care*. Stanford, CA: Stanford University Press.

Brage, E. (2018). "Si no fuera porque me vine …". Itinerarios terapéuticos y prácticas de cuidado en el marco de las migraciones desarrolladas desde el Noroeste y Noreste Argentino hacia la Ciudad Autónoma de Buenos Aires para la atención del cáncer infantil: Un abordaje antropológico. Tesis doctoral. Facultad de Filosofía y Letras, Universidad de Buenos Aires.

Brambilla, C. (2015). Exploring the critical potential of the borderscapes concept. *Geopolitics*, 20(1), 14–34.

Brun, C. (2015). Active waiting and changing hopes: Toward a time perspective on protracted displacement. *Social Analysis*, 59(1), 19–37.

Bunnell, T. (2002). Repositioning Malaysia: High-tech networks and the multicultural rescripting of national identity. *Political Geography*, 21, 105–124.

Burkett, L. (2007). Medical tourism: Concerns, benefits, and the American legal perspective. *The Journal of Legal Medicine*, 28, 223–245.

Buscher, M., & Urry, J. (2009). Mobile methods and the empirical. *European Journal of Social Theory*, 12(1), 99–116.

Button, V. (2000). Legal bid to bypass fertility ruling. *The Age*, 28 August.

Buzinde, C., & Yarnal, C. (2012). Therapeutic landscapes and postcolonial theory: A theoretical approach to medical tourism. *Social Science & Medicine*, 74, 783–787.

Califano, J., Vionnet, E., Pereiro, A., & Nervi, G. (1998). *La cobertura de salud en la Argentina*. Buenos Aires: Premio Bemberg.

Carrillo, R. (1947). Discurso pronunciado por el Secretario de Salud Pública en la comida de camaradería de la Sanidad Nacional. *Archivos de la Secretaría de Salud Pública*, 1(14).

Castañeda, H. (2018). 'Stuck in motion': Simultaneous mobility and immobility in migrant healthcare along the US-Mexico border. In C. Vindrola-Padros, A. Pfister, & G. A. Johnson (eds.), *Healthcare in motion: (Im)mobilities in health service delivery and access* (pp. 19–34). Oxford: Berghahn Books.

Caufield, T., Zarzecny, A., & Toronto Stem Cell Working Group (2012). Stem cell tourism and Canadian family physicians. *Can Fam Physician*, 58, 365–368.

Chalfin, B. (2016). Multiple mobilities and the ethnographic engagement of keywords. In N. Salazar & K. Jayaram (eds.), *Keywords of mobility: Critical engagements* (pp. 171–177). Oxford: Berghahn Books.

Chee, H. (2010). Medical tourism and the state in Malaysia and Singapore. *Global Social Policy*, 10, 336–357.

Chen, Y. B., & Flood, C. (2013). Medical tourism's impact on health care equity and access in low-and middle-income countries: Making the case for regulation. *Journal of Law, Medicine, and Ethics*, 41(1), 286–300.

Coates, J. (2017). Idleness as method: Hairdressers and Chinese urban mobility in Tokyo. In A. Elliot, R. Norum, & N. Salazar (eds.), *Methodologies of mobility: Ethnography and experiment* (pp. 109–128). Oxford: Berghahn Books.

Cohen, E. (2010). Medical travel—a critical assessment. *Tourism Recreation Research*, 35(3), 225–237.

Cohen, G. I. (2015). *Patients with passports: Medical tourism, law and ethics*. Oxford: Oxford University Press.

Collier, S., & Ong, A. (2005). Global assemblages and anthropological problems. In A. Ong & S. Collier (eds.), *Global assemblages: Technology, politics and ethics as anthropological problems* (pp. 3–21). Malden, MA: Blackwell.

Connell, J. (2006). Medical tourism: Sea, sun, sand and ... surgery. *Tourism Management*, 27(6), 1093–1100.

Connell, J. (2010). *Migration and the globalization of health care*. Cheltenham: Edward Elgar.

Connell, J. (2011a). A new inequality? Privatisation, urban bias, migration and medical tourism. *Asia Pacific Viewpoint*, 52(3), 260–271.

Connell, J. (2011b). *Medical tourism*. Wallingford: CABI.

Connell, J. (2013a). Contemporary medical tourism: Conceptualisation, culture and commodification. *Tourism Management*, 34, 1–13.

Connell, J. (2013b). Medical tourism in the Caribbean Islands: A cure for economies in crisis? *Island Studies Journal*, 8(1), 115–130.

Conradson, D., & McKay, D. (2007). Translocal subjectivities: Mobility, connection, emotion. *Mobilities*, 2(2), 167–174.

Cormany, D., & Baloglu, S. (2011). Medical travel facilitator websites: An exploratory study of web page contents and services offered to the prospective medical tourist. *Tourism Management*, 32, 709–716.

Cresswell, T. (2001). The production of mobilities. *New Formations*, 43, 11–25.

Cresswell, T. (2002). *Mobilizing place, placing mobility: The politics of representation in a globalized world*. Amsterdam: Rodopi.Cresswell, T. (2011). Mobilities I: Catching up. *Progress in Human Geography*, 35(4), 550–558.

Crom, D. (1995). The experience of South American mothers who have a child being treated from malignancy in the United States. *Journal of Pediatric Oncology Nursing*, 12(3), 104–112.

Crooks, V., Turner, L., Cohen, G., Bristeir, J., Snyder, J., Casey, V., & Whitmore, R. (2013). Ethical and legal implications for the risks of medical tourism for patients: A qualitative study of Canadian health and safety representatives' perspectives. *BMJ Open*, 3(2), 1–8.

Crooks, V., Whitmore, R., Snyder, J., & Turner, L. (2017). "Ensure that you are well aware of the risks you are taking ...": Actions and activities medical tourists' informal caregivers can undertake to protect their health and safety. *BMC Public Health*, 17, 487.

Dalakoglou, D., & Harvey, P. (2012). Roads and anthropology: Ethnographic perspectives on space, time and (im)mobility. *Mobilities*, 7(4), 459–465.

Dalstrom, M. (2013). Medical travel facilitators: Connecting patients and providers in a globalized world. *Anthropology & Medicine*, 20(1), 24–35.

D'Andrea, A., Ciolfi, L., & Gray, B. (2011). Methodological challenges and innovations in mobilities research. *Mobilities*, 6(2), 149–160.

Davidson, J., Bondi, L., & Smith, M. (2005). *Emotional geographies*. Aldershot: Ashgate.

Day, S. (2015). Waiting and the architecture of care. In V. Das & C. Han (eds.), *Living and dying in the contemporary world: A compendium* (pp. 167–184). Oakland, CA: University of California Press.

Deleuze, G., & Guattari, F. (1994). *What is philosophy?* London: Verso.

Dewsbury, J-D. (2001). The singularity of the 'still': 'Never suspend the question.' In D. Bissell & G. Fuller (eds.), *Stillness in a mobile world* (pp. 175–191). London: Routledge.

Dunn, P. (2007). Medical tourism takes flight. *H and HN: Hospitals and Health Networks*, 40–44.

Edmonds, A. (2011). Almost invisible scars: Medical tourism to Brazil. *Signs*, 36(2), 297–302.

Ehn, B., & Lofgren, O. (2010). *The secret world of doing nothing*. Berkeley, CA: University of California Press.

Einsiedel, E. F., & Adamson, H. (2012). Stem cell tourism and future stem cell tourists: Policy and ethical implications. *Developing World Bioethics*, 12, 35–44.

Eissler, L., & Casken, J. (2013). Seeking health care through international medical tourism. *Journal of Nursing Scholarship*, 45(2), 177–184.

English, V., Mussell, R., Sheather, J., & Sommerville, A. (2005). Ethics briefings. *Journal of Medical Ethics*, 31, 743–744.

Ergler, C., Sakdapolrak, P., Bohle, H., & Kearns, R. (2011). Entitlements to health care: Why is there a preference for private facilities among poorer residents of Chennai, India? *Social Science & Medicine*, 72, 327–337.

Estroff, S. E. (1988). Whose hegemony?: A critical commentary on critical medical anthropology. *Medical Anthropology Quarterly*, 2(4), 421–426.

Eyles, J. (1985). *Sense of place*. Warrington: Silverbrook Press.

Fairchild, S., & Simpson, N. (2004). Mexican migration to the United States Pacific Northwest. *Population Research and Policy Review*, 23(3), 219–234.

Farmer, P. (2003). *Pathologies of power: Health, human rights, and the new war on the poor*. Berkeley, CA: University of California Press.

Fassin, D. (2005). Compassion and repression: The moral economy of immigrant policies in France. *Cultural Anthropology*, 20(3), 362–387.

Flamm, M., & Kaufmann, V. (2006). Operationalising the concept of motility: A qualitative study. *Mobilities*, 1(2), 167–189.

FNDF (2008). *El cáncer pediátrico en la Argentina*. Buenos Aires, Argentina.

FNDF (2009). *Traslados gratuitos y adecuados. Un derecho de los pacientes pediátricos oncológicos*. Fundación Natalí Dafne Flexer, ed. Buenos Aires, Argentina.

FNDF (2010). La Fundación. Electronic document, www.fundacionflexer.org/lafundacion.html, accessed March 2011.

Forgione, D. A., & Smith, P. C. (2007). Medical tourism and its impact on the US health care system. *J Health Care Finance*, 34, 27–35.

Foucault, M. (1963). *The birth of the clinic*. London: Routledge.

Frankenberg, R. (1992). 'Your time or mine': Temporal contradictions of biomedical practice. In F. Ronald (ed.), *Time, health and medicine* (pp. 1–30). London: SAGE.

Garcia-Altes, A. (2005). The development of health tourism services. *Annals of Tourism Research*, 32(1), 266–268.

Gask, L., Aseem, S., Waquas, A., & Waheed, W. (2011). Isolation, feeling 'stuck' and loss of control: Understanding persistence of depression in British Pakistani women. *Journal of Affective Disorders*, 128(1), 49–55.

Gatrell, A., & Elliott, S. (2009). *Geographies of health: An introduction*. Malden, MA: Wiley-Blackwell.

Gesler, W. (1993). Therapeutic landscapes: Theory and a case study of Epidauros, Greece. *Environment and Planning D: Society and Space*, 11(2), 171–189.

Gesler, W. M. (1996). Lourdes: Healing in a place of pilgrimage. *Health and Place*, 2, 95–105.

Geertz, C. (2000). *Available light: Anthropological reflections on philosophical topics*. Princeton, NJ: Princeton University Press.

Ginsburg, F., & Rapp, R. (1991). The politics of reproduction. *Annual Review of Anthropology*, 20, 311–343.

Glick Schiller, N., & Salazar, N. B. (2013). Regimes of mobility across the globe. *Journal of Ethnic and Migration Studies*, 39(2), 183–200.

Golbert, L. (2000). The social agenda in Argentina: A review of retirement and employment policies. In J. S. Tulchin & A. M. Garland (eds.), *Social development in Latin America: The politics of reform* (pp. 227–242). Boulder, CO: Lynne Rienner Pub.

Goodrich, J. (1993). Socialist Cuba: A study of health tourism. *Journal of Travel Research*, 32(1), 36–42.

Green, S. (2013). Borders and the relocation of Europe. *Annual Review of Anthropology*, 42, 345–361.

Green, P. (2016). Biomedicine and 'risky' retirement destinations: Older Western residents in Ubud, Bali. *Medical Anthropology*, 35(2), 147–160.

Guarneri, V., Barbieri, E., Dieci, M., Piacentini, F., & Conte, P. (2011). Timing for starting second-line therapy in recurrent ovarian cancer. *Expert Review of Anticancer Therapy*, 11(1), 49–55.

Gubrium, J., & Holstein, J. (2009). *Analyzing narrative reality*. Los Angeles, CA: SAGE.

Gürtin, Z. B. (2012). IVF practitioners as interface agents between the local and the global: The localization of IVF in Turkey. In M. Knect, M. Klotz, & S. Beck. (eds.), *Reproductive technologies as global form*. Frankfurt: Campus Verlag.

Habeck, J., & Broz, L. (2015). Introduction: Experience and emotion in Northern mobilities. *Mobilities*, 10(4), 511–517.

Habermas, J. (1970). Technology and science as 'ideology.' In N. Stehr & R. Grundmann (eds.), *Knowledge: Critical concepts*. London: Routledge.

Hadler, M. (2015). Migration and patient mobility in Latin America. In N. Lunt, D. Horsfall, & J. Hanefeld (eds.), *Handbook on medical tourism and patient mobility* (pp. 313–322). Cheltenham: Edward Elgar.

Hage, G. (ed.) (2009). *Waiting*. Melbourne: Melbourne University Press.

Hall, C. M., & James, M. (2011). Medical tourism: Emerging biosecurity and nosocomial issues. *Tourism Review*, 66, 118–126.

Hampshire, K. R., Porter, G., Asiedu Owusu, S., Tanle, A., & Abane, A. (2011). Out of the reach of children? Young people's health-seeking practices and agency in Africa's newly-emerging therapeutic landscapes. *Social Science and Medicine*, 73, 702–710.

Hannam, K., Sheller, M., & Urry, J. (2006). Editorial: Mobilities, immobilities and moorings. *Mobilities*, 1(1), 1–22.

Harrison, P. (2001). The broken thread: On being still. In D. Bissell & G. Fuller (eds.), *Stillness in a mobile world* (pp. 209–228). London: Routledge.

Harvey, D. (1989). *The condition of postmodernity*. Oxford: Blackwell.

Harvey, P., & Knox, H. (2012). The enchantments of infrastructure. *Mobilities*, 7(4), 521–536.

Hazarika, I. (2010). Medical tourism: Its potential impact on the health workforce and health systems in India. *Health Policy and Planning*, 25, 248–251.

Helble, M. (2011). The movement of patients across borders: Challenges and opportunities for public health. *Bulletin World Health Organization*, 89, 68–72.

Heng Leng, C. (2010). Medical tourism and the state in Malaysia and Singapore. *Global Social Policy*, 10, 336–357.

Heng Leng, C. & Whittaker, A. (2010). Guest editors' introduction to the special issue: Why is medical travel of concern to global social policy? *Global Social Policy*, 10, 287–291.

Higginbotham, G. (2011). Assisted-suicide tourism: Is it tourism? *Tourismos: An International Multidisciplinary Journal of Tourism*, 6, 177–185.

Hopkins, L., Labonte, R., Runnels, V., & Packer, C. (2010). Medical tourism today: What is the state of existing knowledge? *Journal of Public Health Policy*, 31(2), 185–198.

Horowitz, M., & Rosensweig, J. (2007). Medical tourism – health care in the global economy. *The Physician Executive*, 24–30.

Horsfall, D., & Lunt, N. (2016). Medical tourism by numbers. In N. Lunt, D. Horsfall, & J. Hanefled (eds.), *Handbook on medical tourism and patient mobility* (pp. 25–36). Cheltenham: Edward Elgar.

Howard, S., Pedrosa, M., Lins, M., Pedrosa, A. Pui, C-H., Ribeiro, R., & Pedrosa, F. (2004). Establishment of a pediatric oncology program and outcomes of childhood acute lymphoblastic leukemia in a resource-poor area. *JAMA*, 291(20), 2471–2475.

Hunter, D., & Oultram, S. (2008). The challenge of sperm ships: The need for global regulation of medical technology. *Journal of Medical Ethics*, 34, 552–556.

Hunter, D., & Oultram, S. (2010). The ethical and policy implications of rogue medical tourism. *Global Social Policy*, 10, 297–299.

INDEC (2005). Artículos de la convención sobre los derechos del niño y de la ley 26.061 referidos a los derechos a la vida y a la salud.

Inhorn, M. (1996). *Infertility and patriarchy: The cultural politics of gender and family life in Egypt*. Philadelphia, PA: University of Pennsylvania Press.

Inhorn, M. (2003). *Local babies, global science: Gender, religion and in-vitro fertilization in Egypt*. New York: Routledge.

Inhorn, M. (2007). Masculinity, reproduction and male infertility surgeries in Egypt and Lebanon. *Journal of Middle East Women's Studies*, 3(3), 1–20.

Inhorn, M. (2008). Islam, assisted reproductive technologies, and the Middle Eastern state. *Babylon: Norwegian Journal of the Middle East*, 6, 32–43.

Inhorn, M. (2011). Diasporic dreaming: Return reproductive tourism to the Middle East. *Reproductive BioMedicine Online*, 23(5), 582–591.

Inhorn, M. (2015). *Cosmopolitan conceptions: IVF sojourns in global Dubai*. Durham, NC: Duke University Press.

Jayaram, K. (2016). Capital. In N. Salazar & K. Jayaram (eds.), *Keywords of mobility: Critical engagements* (pp. 13–32). Oxford: Berghahn Books.

Jenner, E. (2008). Unsettled borders of care: Medical tourism as a new dimension in America's health care crisis. *Research in the Sociology of Health Care*, 26, 235–249.

Jensen, A. (2011). Mobility, space and power: On the multiplicities of seeing mobility. *Mobilities*, 6(2), 255–271.

Jensen, O. (2013). *Staging mobilities*. London: Routledge.

Jensen, O. (2014). *Designing mobilities*. Aalborg: Aalborg University Press.

Johnston, R., Crooks, V. A., Snyder, J., & Kingsbury, P. (2010). What is known about the effects of medical tourism in destination and departure countries? A scoping review. *International Journal for Equity in Health*, 9(24), 1–13.

Johnston, R., Crooks, V. A., & Snyder, J. (2012). "I didn't even know what I was looking for": A qualitative study of the decision-making processes of Canadian medical tourists. *Globalization and Health*, 8(3), 1–12.

Kangas, B. (2002). Therapeutic itineraries in a global world: Yemenis and their search for biomedical treatment abroad. *Medical Anthropology*, 21(1), 35–78.

Kangas, B. (2007). Hope from abroad in the international medical travel of Yemeni patients. *Anthropology and Medicine*, 14(3), 293–305.

Kangas, B. (2010). Traveling for medical care in a global world. *Medical Anthropology*, 29(4), 344–362.

Kangas, B. (2011). Complicating common ideas about medical tourism: Gender, class, and globality in Yemeni's international medical travel. *Signs*, 36(2), 327–332.

Kassim, P. (2009). Medicine beyond borders: The legal and ethical challenges. *Med Law*, 28, 439–450.

Katz, I. (1998). *Al gran pueblo Argentino salud!: Una propuesta operativa integradora*. Buenos Aires: Eudeba.

Katz, I. (2004). *Argentina hospital: El rostro oscuro de la salud*. Buenos Aires: Edhasa.

Katz, J., & Muñoz, A. (1988). *Organización del sector salud: Puja distributiva y equidad*. Buenos Aires: Bibliotecas Universitarias, CEPAL.

Kaufmann, V. (2002). *Re-thinking mobility. Contemporary Sociology*. Aldershot: Ashgate.

Kaufmann, V., Manfred, B., & Dominique, J. (2004). Motility: Mobility as capital. *International Journal of Urban and Regional Research*, 28(4), 745–756.

Kearney, M. (1995). The local and the global: The anthropology of globalization and transnationalism. *Annual Review of Anthropology*, 24, 547–565.

Kearns, R. (1993). Place and health: Toward a reformed medical geography. *The Professional Geographer*, 45, 139–147.

Kearns, R., & Collins, D. (2010). Health geography. In T. Brown, S. McLafferty, & G. Moon (eds.), *A companion to health and medical geography* (pp. 15-32). Malden, MA: Wiley-Blackwell.

Kearns, R., & Gesler, W. (1998). Introduction. In R. Kearns & W. Gesler (eds.), *Putting health into place: Landscape, identity, and wellbeing* (pp. 1-13). New York: Syracuse University Press.

Keckley, P. H., & Underwood, H. R. (2008). *Medical tourism: Update and implications.* Washington, D.C.: Deloitte Center for Health Solutions.

Kellerman, A. (2012). Potential mobilities. *Mobilities*, 7(1), 171-183.

Khan, N. (2016). Immobility. In N. Salazar & K. Jayaram (eds.), *Keywords of mobility: Critical engagements* (pp. 93-112). Oxford: Berghahn Books.

Klaus, M. (2006). Outsourcing vital operations: What if US health care costs drive patients overseas for surgery? *Quinnipiac Health Law Journal*, 9(219), 235-237.

Knodel, J., & VanLandingham, M. (2003). Return migration in the context of parental assistance in the AIDS epidemic: The Thai experience. *Social Science and Medicine*, 57, 327-342.

Kohn, A., & Aguero, A. (1985). El contexto medico. In H. Biagini (ed.), *El Movimiento Positivista*. Buenos Aires: Editorial de Belgrano.

Korpela, M. (2016). Infrastructures. In N. Salazar & K. Jayaram (eds.), *Keywords of mobility: Critical engagements* (pp. 113-132). Oxford: Berghahn Books.

Lanfrant, M. (1995). Introduction. In M-F. Lanfrant, J. Allcock, & E. Bruner (eds.), *International tourism: Identity and change* (pp. 1-23). London: SAGE.

Larsen, J., & Urry, J. (2008). Networking in mobile societies. In J. O. Bærenholdt, B. Granås, & S. Kesselring (eds.), *Mobility and place: Enacting Northern European peripheries* (pp. 89-101). Aldershot: Ashgate.

Larsen, J., Urry, J., & Axhausen, K. (2006). *Mobilities, networks, geographies.* Aldershot: Ashgate.

Laurier, E. et al. (2008). Driving and "passengering": Notes on the ordinary organization of car travel. *Mobilities*, 3, 1-23.

Le Compte, M., & Schensul, J. (2013). *Analysis and interpretation of ethnographic data: A mixed methods approach.* Lanham, MD: Altamira.

Leahy, A. L. (2008). Medical tourism: The impact of travel to foreign countries for healthcare. *Surgeon*, 6(5), 260–261.

Lean, G., Staiff, R., & Waterton, E. (2014). *Travel and imagination*. Farnham: Ashgate.

Lee, J. Y., Kearns, R. A., & Friesen, W. (2010). Seeking affective health care: Korean immigrants' use of homeland medical services. *Health & Place*, 16, 108–115.

Leivestad, H. H. (2016). Motility. In N. Salazar & K. Jayaram (eds.), *Keywords of mobility: Critical engagements* (pp. 133–151). Oxford: Berghahn Books.

Lin, W., Lindquist, J., Xiang, B., & Yeoh, B. S. A. (2017). Migration infrastructures and the production of migrant mobilities. *Mobilities*, 12(2), 167–174.

Lindquist, J. (2009). *The anxieties of mobility: Migration and tourism in the Indonesian Borderlands*. Honolulu, HI: Hawaii University Press.

Lipovec, U. (2008). The metastasis of erasure. In J. Zorn & U. Lipovec (eds.), *Once upon an erasure: From citizens to illegal residents in the Republic of Slovenia* (pp. 71–88). Slovenia: Študentska založba.

Lloyd-Sherlock, P. (2002). Health, equity and social exclusion in Argentina and Mexico. In C. Abel & C. Lewis (eds.), *Exclusion and engagement: Social policy in Latin America* (pp. 172–188). London: Institute of Latin American Studies, University of London.

Low, S., & Lawrence-Zuniga, D. (2003). Locating culture. In S. Low & D. Lawrence-Zuniga (eds.), *The anthropology of space and culture: Locating culture* (pp. 1–47). Malden, MA: Blackwell Publishing.

Lunt, N., & Carrera, P. (2010). Medical tourism: Assessing the evidence on treatment abroad. *Maturitas*, 66, 27–32.

Lunt, N., & Mannion, R. (2014). Patient mobility in the global marketplace: A multidisciplinary perspective. *IJHPM*, 2(4), 155–157.

Lunt, N., Horsfall, D., & Hanefeld, J. (eds.) (2015). *Handbook on medical tourism and patient mobility*. Cheltenham: Edward Elgar.

Mackenzie, A. (2002). *Transductions: Bodies and machines at speed*. London/New York: Continuum.

Manderscheid, K. (2009). Unequal mobilities. In T. Ohnmacht, H. Maksim, & M. M. Bergman (eds.), *Mobilities and inequality* (pp. 27–50). Aldershot: Ashgate.

Manderscheid, K. (2014). The movement problem, the car and future mobility regimes: Automobility as dispositif and mode of regulation. *Mobilities*, 9(4), 604–626.

Marcus, G. (1995). Ethnography in/of the world system: The emergence of multi-sited ethnography. *Annual Review of Anthropology*, 24, 95–97.

Martin, D. (2010). Ethical issues in medical travel for human biological materials. *Global Social Policy*, 10, 3.

Martinez Alvarez, M., Chanda, R., & Smith, R. (2011). The potential for bi-lateral agreements in medical tourism: A qualitative study of stakeholder perspectives from the UK and India. *Globalization and Health*, 7, 11.

Massey, D. (1991). A global sense of place. In S. Daniels & R. Lee (eds.), *Exploring human geography* (pp. 237–245). London: Arnold.

Meghani, Z. (2011). A robust, particularist ethical assessment of medical tourism. *Developing World Bioethics*, 11(1), 16–29.

Mera, J. & Ruiz del Castillo, R. (2000). *La reforma de salud en el tercer milenio*. Buenos Aires: Editorial Dunken.

Mertnoff, R., Vindrola-Padros, C., Jacobs, M., & Gómez-Batiste, X. (2017). The development of palliative care in Argentina: A mapping study using Latin American Association for Palliative Care indicators. *Journal of Palliative Medicine*, 20(8), 829–837.

Meroni, R. (1982). Historia de la Pediatría Clínica. In *Primer Congreso Hispanoamericano de Historia de la Medicina*. Buenos Aires: Asociación Medica Argentina, Sociedad Argentina de la Historia de la Medicina.

Merriman, P. (2016). Mobility infrastructures: Modern visions, affective environments and the problem of car parking. *Mobilities*, 11(1), 83–98.

Milligan, C. (2007). Restoration or risk? Exploring the place of the common place. In A. Williams (ed.), *Therapeutic landscapes*. Aldershot: Ashgate.

Milstein, A., & Smith, M. (2006). America's new refugees—seeking affordable surgery offshore. *New England Journal of Medicine*, 355, 1637–1640.

Ministerio de Salud. (2010). Indicadores Basicos. Buenos Aires, Argentina. www.deis.msal.gov.ar/wp-content/uploads/2018/04/indicadores_2010.pdf

Mirrer-Singer, P. M. (2007). Medical malpractice overseas: The legal uncertainty surrounding medical tourism. *Law Contemp Probl*, 70, 211–232.

Mol, A. (2008). *The logic of care: Health and the problem of patient choice.* London: Routledge.

Moreno, F. (2007). *Cuando sospechar cáncer en el nino?* Buenos Aires: ROHA and Fundación Hospital Garrahan.

Moreno, F., Schvartzman, E., Scopinaro, M., Diez, B., Garcia Lombardi, M., Loria, D., de Davila, M. T., Kumcher, I., & Goldman, J. (2009). *Registro Oncopediátrico Hospitalario Argentino (ROHA). Resultados 2000-2008.* Buenos Aires: Ministerio de Salud.

Moreno, F., Dussel, V., Abriata, G., Loria, D., & Orellana, L. (2013). *Registro Oncopediátrico Hospitalario Argentino (ROHA).* Buenos Aires: Ministerio de Salud.

Morley, D. (2002). *Home territories: Media, mobility and identity.* London: Routledge.

Murphy-Lejeune, E. (2002). *Student mobility and narrative in Europe: The new strangers.* London: Routledge.

Nari, M. (1996). Las Practicas anticonceptivas, la disminución de la natalidad y el debate medico, 1890-1940. In M. Lobato (ed.), *Política, médicos y enfermedades* (pp. 153-189). Buenos Aires: Editorial Biblos.

Nolan, J. M., & Schneider, M. J. (2011). Medical tourism in the backcountry: Alternative health and healing in the Arkansas Ozarks. *Signs,* 36(2), 319-326.

Olaviaga, S., & Maceira, D. (2007). Mapa de actores del sector oncológico en la Argentina. *CIPPEC Políticas Publicas Análisis,* 37, 1-11.

Olivier de Sardan, J. (1995). La politique du terrain: Sur la production des données en anthropologie. *Enquête,* 1, 71-109.

Ong, A. (1999). *Flexible citizenship: The cultural logics of transnationality.* Durham, NC: Duke University Press.

Ong, A. (2005). Economies of expertise: Assembling flows, managing citizenship. In A. Ong & S. Collier (eds.), *Global assemblages: Technology, politics and ethics as anthropological problems* (pp. 337-353). Malden, MA: Blackwell.

Ormond, M. (2011). Shifting subjects of health-care: Placing 'medical tourism' in the context of Malaysian domestic health-care reform. *Asia Pacific Viewpoint,* 52(3), 247-259.

Ormond, M. (2013). *Neoliberal governance and international medical travel in Malaysia*. London: Routledge.

Ormond, M. (2015a). En route: Transport and embodiment in international medical travel journeys between Indonesia and Malaysia. *Mobilities*, 10(2), 285–303.

Ormond, M. (2015b). Government and governance strategies in medical tourism. In N. Lunt, D. Horsfall, & J. Hanefeld (eds.), *Handbook on medical tourism and patient mobility* (pp. 154–163). Cheltenham: Edward Elgar.

Österlund-Pötzsch, S. (2017). 'Few are the roads I haven't travelled': Mobility as method in early Finland-Swedish ethnographic expeditions. In A. Elliot, R. Norum, & N. Salazar (eds.), *Methodologies of mobility: Ethnography and experiment* (pp. 1–24). Oxford: Berghahn Books.

Pachanee, C., & Wibulpolprasert, S. (2006). Incoherent policies on universal coverage of health insurance and promotion of international trade in health services in Thailand. *Health Policy and Planning*, 21(4), 310–318.

Pachanee, C. (2009). Implications on public health from Mode 2 trade in health services: Empirical evidence. Report available at: http://ihppthaigov.net/DB/publication/attachresearch/245/chapter1.pdf

Pafford, B. (2009). The third wave—medical tourism in the 21st century. *South Med J*, 102(8), 810–813.

Pannarunothai, S. et al. (1998). *Management of public and private hospitals: A financial and business opportunities for the autonomous hospitals*. Nonthaburi: Health Systems Research Institute.

Parkin, D. (2014). Pathways to healing: Curative travel among Muslims and non-Muslims in Eastern East Africa. *Medical Anthropology*, 33, 21–36.

Parks, J. (2010). Care ethics and the global practice of commercial surrogacy. *Bioethics*, 24, 323–332.

Pelto, P. (1988). A note on critical medical anthropology. *Medical Anthropology Quarterly*, 2(4), 435–437.

Penney, K., Snyder, J., Crooks, V., & Johnston, R. (2011). Risk communication and informed consent in the medical tourism industry: A thematic content analysis of Canadian broker websites. *BMC Medical Ethics*, 12(17), 1–9.

Pennings, G. (2004). Legal harmonization and reproductive tourism in Europe. *Human Reproduction*, 19, 2689–2694.

Pennings, G. (2007). Ethics without boundaries: Medical tourism. In R. E. Ashcroft, A. Dawson, H. Draper, & J. R. McMillan (eds.), *Principles of health care ethics* (pp. 505–510). Chichester: John Wiley & Sons.

Pennings, G. (2015). Ethics of medical tourism. In N. Lunt, D. Horsfall, & J. Hanefeld (eds.), *Handbook on medical tourism and patient mobility* (pp. 341–349). Cheltenham: Edward Elgar Publishing.

Perfetto, R., & Dholakia, N. (2010). Exploring the cultural contradictions of medical tourism. *Consumption Markets & Culture*, 13(4), 399–417.

Pieke, F. (1999). Introduction: Chinese and European perspectives on migration. In F. Pieke & Mallee, H. (eds.), *Internal and international migration: Chinese perspectives* (pp. 1–26). Richmond: Curzon Press.

Pink, S., Kurti, L., & Alfonso, A. (eds.) (2004). *Working images: Visual research and representation in ethnography*. London: Routledge.

Plotnikova, E. (2018). Governing mobility of health workers across borders: From local to global policy tools. In C. Vindrola-Padros, A. Pfister, & G. A. Johnson (eds.), *Healthcare in motion: (Im)mobilities in health service delivery and access* (pp. 116–138). Oxford: Berghahn Books.

Pocock, N., & Phua, K. (2011). Medical tourism and policy implications for health systems: A conceptual framework from a comparative study of Thailand, Singapore and Malaysia. *Globalization and Health*, 7, 1–12.

Politi, P. (2001). *Objeciones fundadas a la propuesta de protocolos nacionales de oncología* Clínica del Ministerio de Salud.

Ramirez de Arellano, A. (2007). Patients without borders: The emergence of medical tourism. *International Journal of Health Services*, 37(1), 193–198.

Ringrose, J., & Coleman, R. (2013). Looking and desiring machines: A feminist Deleuzian mapping of bodies and affects. In R. Coleman (ed.), *Deleuze and research methodologies* (pp. 125–145). Edinburgh: Edinburgh University Press.

Rodriguez, J. (2006). *Civilizing Argentina: Science, medicine and the modern state*. Chapel Hill, NC: University of North Carolina Press.

ROHA (Registro Oncopediatrico Hospitalario Argentino). (2008). *Resultados 2000-2008*. Buenos Aires: ROHA, Fundacion Kaleidos.

ROHA (Registro Oncopediatrico Hospitalario Argentino). (2018). *Resultados 2000-2016*. Buenos Aires: ROHA, Fundacion Kaleidos.

Romero-Ortuño, R. (2004). Access to health care for illegal immigrants in the EU: Should we be concerned? *European Journal of Health Law*, 11, 245–272.

Ruggiero, K. (2004). *Modernity in the flesh: Medicine, law, and society in turn-of-the-century Argentina*. Stanford, CA: Stanford University Press.

Rumford, C. (2006). Theorizing borders. *European Journal of Social Theory*, 9(2), 155–169.

Runnels, V., & Carrera, P. (2012). Why do patients engage in medical tourism? *Maturitas*, 73, 300–304.

Sager, T. (2006). Freedom as mobility: Implications of the distinction between actual and potential travelling. *Mobilities*, 1(3), 465–488.

Salazar, N. (2010a). *Envisioning Eden: Mobilizing imaginaries in tourism and beyond*. Oxford: Berghahn Books.

Salazar, N. (2010b). Towards an anthropology of cultural mobilities. *Crossings: Journal of Migration and Culture*, 1, 53–68.

Salazar, N. (2011). The power of imagination in transnational mobilities. *Identities*, 18(6), 576–598.

Salazar, N. (2012). Tourism imaginaries: A conceptual approach. *Annals of Tourism Research*, 39(2), 863–882.

Salazar, N. (2013). Imagining mobility at the end of the world. *History and Anthropology*, 24(2), 233–252.

Salazar, N. (2016). Keywords of mobility. What's in a name? In N. Salazar & K. Jayaram (eds.), *Keywords of mobility: Critical engagements* (pp. 1–12). Oxford: Berghahn Books.

Salazar, N. B., & Smart, A. (2011). Anthropological takes on (im)mobility. In N. Salazar & A. Smart (eds.), *Identities: Global studies in culture and power* (pp. i–ix). London/New York: Routledge.

Salazar, N. B., Elliot, A., & Norum, R. (2017). Studying mobilities: Theoretical notes and methodological queries. In A. Elliot, R. Norum, & N. Salazar (eds.), *Methodologies of mobility: Ethnography and experiment* (pp. 1–24). Oxford: Berghahn Books.

Saniotis, A. (2007). Changing ethics in medical practice: A Thai perspective. *Indian Journal of Medical Ethics*, 4(1), 24–25.

Scambler, G. (2013). *Habermas, critical theory and health*. London: Routledge.

Scheper-Hughes, N. (1990). Three propositions for a critically applied medical anthropology. *Social Science and Medicine*, 30(2), 189–198.

Sheller, M., & Urry, J. (2006). The new mobilities paradigm. *Environment and Planning A*, 38, 207–226.

Simmel, G. (1997). *Simmel on culture*. Frisby, D., Featherstone, M., (eds.). London: SAGE.

Singer, M. (1989). The limitations of medical ecology: The concept of adaptation in the context of social stratification and social transformation. *Medical Anthropology*, 10, 223–234.

Singer, M. (1990). Introduction. Critical medical anthropology in question. *Social Science and Medicine*, 30(2), V–VIII.

Singer, M. (1995). Beyond the ivory tower: Critical praxis in medical anthropology. *Medical Anthropology Quarterly*, 9(1), 80–106.

Singer, M., & Baer, H. (2018). *Critical medical anthropology*. London: Routledge.

Skeggs, B. (2004). *Class, self, culture*. London: Routledge.

Smith, E., Behrmann, J., Martin, C., & Williams-Jones, B. (2009). Reproductive tourism in Argentina: Clinic accreditation and its implications for consumers, health professionals, and policy makers. *Developing World Bioethics*, 10(2), 59–69.

Smith, R., Martinez-Alvarez, M., & Chanda, R. (2011). Medical tourism: A review of the literature and analysis of a role for bi-lateral trade. *Health Policy*, 103, 276–282.

Smith, K. (2012). The problematization of medical tourism: A critique of neoliberalism. *Bioethics*, 12(1), 1–8.

Snyder, J., Crooks, V. A., Johnston, R., & Kingsbury, P. (2011). What do we know about Canadian involvement in medical tourism? A scoping review. *Open Med*, 5, 139–148.

Snyder, J., Crooks, V., Turner, L., & Johnston, R. (2013). Understanding the impacts of medical tourism on health human resources in Barbados: A prospective, qualitative study of stakeholder perceptions. *International Journal of Equity in Health*, 12, 2–11.

Sobo, E. (2009). Medical travel: What it means, why it matters. *Medical Anthropology*, 28, 326–335.

Sobo, E. (2015). Culture and medical travel. In N. Lunt, D. Horsfall, & J. Hanefeld (eds.), *Handbook on medical tourism and patient mobility* (pp. 217–227). Cheltenham: Edward Elgar.

Sobo, E., Herlihy, E., & Bicker, M. (2011). Selling medical travel to US patient-consumers: The cultural appeal of website marketing messages. *Anthropology and Medicine*, 18(1), 119–136.

Soderström, O., Ruedin, D., Randeria, S, D'Amato, G., & Panese, F. (eds.) (2013). *Critical mobilities*. London: Routledge.

Solomon, H. (2011). Affective journeys: The emotional structuring of medical tourism in India. *Anthropology and Medicine*, 18, 105–118.

Song, P. (2010). Biotech pilgrims and the transnational quest for stem cell cures. *Medical Anthropology*, 29(4), 384–402.

Song, P. (2017). *Biomedical odysseys: Fetal cell experiments from cyberspace to China*. Princeton, NJ: Princeton University Press.

Speier, A. (2011). Brokers, consumers and the Internet: How North American consumers navigate their infertility journeys. *Reproductive Biomedicine Online*, 23(5), 592–599.

Speier, A. (2016). *Fertility holidays: IVF tourism and the reproduction of whiteness*. New York: New York University Press.

Spinney, J. (2011). A chance to catch a breath: Using mobile video ethnography in cycling research. *Mobilities*, 6(2), 161–182.

Spinoza, B. (2001). *Ethics*. Wadsworth.

Star, S. L. (1999). The ethnography of infrastructure. *American Behavioral Scientist*, 43(3), 377–391.

Stawski, M. E. (2009). *Asistencia social y buenos negocios: Politica de la Fundacion Eva Peron, 1948–1955*. Buenos Aires: Imago Mundi.

Stephano, R. (2012). The Dominican Republic for health, wellness and luxury. *Medical Tourism Magazine*, 26, 53–55.

Storrow, R. (2005). Quests for conception: Fertility tourists, globalization and feminist legal theory. *Hastings Legal Journal*, 57, 295–330.

Szakolczai, A. (2009). Liminality and experience: Structuring transitory situations and transformative events. *International Political Anthropology*, 2, 141–172.

Tesfahuney, M. (1998). Mobility, racism and geopolitics. *Political Geography*, 17(5), 499–515.

Thompson, A. (ed.) (1995). *Público y privado: Las organizaciones sin fines de lucro en la Argentina*. Buenos Aires: UNICEF/Losada.

Thrift, N. (2004). Movement-space: The changing domain of thinking resulting from the development of new kinds of spatial awareness. *Economy and Society*, 33(4), 582–604.

Thrift, N., & French, S. (2002). The automatic production of space. *Transactions of the Institute of British Geographers*, 27(3), 309–335.

Tobar, F., Olaviaga, S., & Solano, R. (2011). Retos postergados y nuevos desafios del Sistema de salud Argentino. *CIPPEC, Documento de Politicas Publicas*, 99, 1–15.

Toziano, R., Walter, R., Brulc, A., Navia, M., Quintana, S., & Flores, A. (2004). Perfil sociodemográfico y de la atención de pacientes oncológicos provenientes de cinco provincias en un hospital de atención terciaria. *Archivos Argentinos de Pediatria*, 102(4), 301–307.

Tsing, A. (2005). *Friction: An ethnography of global connection*. Princeton, NJ: Princeton University Press.

Turner, L. (2007). First world care at third world prices: Globalization, bioethics and medical tourism. *Biosocieties*, 2, 303–325.

Turner, L. (2011). Canadian medical tourism companies that have exited the marketplace: Content analysis of websites used to market transnational medical travel. *Globalization and Health*, 7(40).

Ugalde, A., Homedes, N., & Zwi, A. (2002). Globalisation, equity and health in Latin America. In C. Abel & C. Lewis (eds.), *Exclusion and engagement: Social policy in Latin America* (pp. 151–171). London: Institute of Latin American Studies, University of London.

Urry, J. (2000). *Sociology beyond societies*. London: Routledge.

Urry, J. (2002). Mobility and proximity. *Sociology*, 36(2), 255–274.

Urry, J. (2003). *Global complexity*. Cambridge: Polity.

Urry, J. (2007). *Mobilities*. Cambridge: Polity Press.

Uteng, T., & Cresswell, T. (2008). *Gendered mobilities*. Aldershot: Ashgate.

Van Andel, P. (1994). Serendipity: Origin, history, domains, traditions, appearances, patterns and programmability. *The British Journal for the Philosophy of Science*, 45(2), 631–679.

Van der Geest, S., & Finkler, K. (2004). Hospital ethnography: Introduction. *Social Science & Medicine*, 59(10), 1995–2001.

Van Hoof, W., & Pennings, G. (2018). Ethical problems related to legal diversity: Limiting access for non-resident patients in cross-border reproductive care. In R. Ryan-Flood & J. Gunnarsson Payne (eds.), *Transnationalising reproduction: Third party conception in a globalized world* (pp. 141–151). Abingdon: Routledge.

Van Hoof, W., Pennings, G., & De Sutter, P. (2016). Cross-border reproductive care for law evasion: Should physicians be allowed to help infertility patients evade the law of their own country? *European Journal of Obstetrics & Gynecology and Reproductive Biology*, 202, 101–105.

Vergunst, J. (2011). Technology and technique in a useful ethnography of movement. *Mobilities*, 6(2), 203–219.

Veronelli, J. C., & Veronelli, M. (2004). *Los orígenes de las instituciones de la salud publica en la Argentina*. Buenos Aires: Organización Panamericana de la Salud (OPS).

Verstraete, G., & Cresswell, T. (eds.) (2002). *Mobilizing place, placing mobility*. Amsterdam: Rodopi.

Viladrich, A., & Baron-Faust, R. (2014). Medical tourism in tango paradise: The internet branding of cosmetic surgery in Argentina. *Annals of Tourism Research*, 45, 116–131.

Vindrola-Padros, C. (2009). *The participation of NGOs in healthcare. The case of pediatric cancer treatment in Argentina*. MA thesis. Department of Anthropology, University of South Florida.

Vindrola-Padros, C. (2011). *Life and death journeys: Medical travel, cancer and children in Argentina*. PhD thesis. Department of Anthropology, University of South Florida.

Vindrola-Padros, C. (2012). The everyday lives of children with cancer in Argentina: Going beyond the disease and treatment. *Children and Society*, 26, 430–442.

Vindrola-Padros, C. (2015). A cautionary tale: The 'new' medical tourism industry in Argentina. *Somatechnics*, 5(1), 69–87.

Vindrola-Padros, C. (forthcoming). *Carework and medical travel: Exploring the emotional dimensions of caring on the move.*

Vindrola-Padros, C., & Brage, E. (2017). Child medical travel in Argentina: Narratives of family separation and moving away from home. In C. R. Ergler & R. A. Kearnes (eds.), *Children's health and wellbeing in urban environments*. London: Routledge.

Vindrola-Padros, C., & Johnson, G. A. (2015). Children seeking health care: International perspectives on children's use of mobility to obtain health services. In A. White, C. Ni Laoire, & T. Skelton (eds.), *Movement, mobilities and journeys: Geographies of children and young people series*, Vol. 6, Springer.

Vindrola-Padros, C., & Whiteford, L. M. (2012). The search for medical technologies abroad: The case of medical travel and pediatric oncology treatment in Argentina. *Technology and Innovation*, 14, 25–38.

Vindrola-Padros, C., Johnson, G., & Pfister, A. (2018). *Healthcare in motion: Immobilities in health service delivery and access*. New York: Berghahn Books.

Vindrola-Padros, C., Vindrola-Padros, B., & Lee-Crossett, K. (eds.) (forthcoming). *Immobility and medicine: Exploring stillness, emptiness and the in-between.* Palgrave Macmillan.

Wagner, H. P., & Antic, V. (1997). The problem of pediatric malignancies in the developing world. *Annals of the New York Academy of Sciences*, 824, 193–204.

Waitzkin, H. (1991). *The politics of medical encounters: How patients and doctors deal with social problems*. New Haven, CT: Yale University Press.

Warf, B. (2010). Do you know the way to San Jose? Medical tourism in Costa Rica. *Journal of Latin American Geography*, 9(1), 51–66.

White, N. R., & White, P. B. (2004). Travel as transition: Identity and place. *Annals of Tourism Research*, 31(1), 200–218.

Whiteford, L., & Whiteford, S. (2005). *Globalization, water, & health: Resource management in times of scarcity.* Santa Fe, NM: School of American Research Press.

Whitehead, M. (1991). The concepts and principles of equity and health. *Health Promotion International,* 6(3), 217–228.

Whittaker, A. (2008). Pleasure and pain: Medical travel in Asia. *Global Public Health,* 3(3), 271–290.

Whittaker, A. (2010). Challenges of medical travel to global regulation: A case study of reproductive travel in Asia. *Global Social Policy,* 10(3), 396–415.

Whittaker, A. (2011). Cross-border assisted reproduction care in Asia: Implications for access, equity and regulations. *Reproductive Health Matters,* 19(37), 107–116.

Whittaker, A., & Chee H. (2015). Perceptions of an 'international hospital' in Thailand by medical travel patients: Cross-cultural tensions in a transnational space. *Social Science & Medicine,* 124, 290–297.

Whittaker, A., & Speier, A. (2010). "Cycling overseas": Care, commodification, and stratification in cross-border reproductive travel. *Medical Anthropology,* 29(4), 363–383.

Whittaker, A., Manderson, L., & Cartwright, E. (2010). Patients without borders: Understanding medical travel. *Medical Anthropology,* 29, 336–343.

Wibulpolprasert, S., & Pachanee, C. (2008). Addressing the internal brain drain of medical doctors in Thailand: The story and lesson learned. *Global Social Policy,* 8, 12–15.

Wibulpolprasert, S., & Pengpaibon, P. (2003). Integrated strategies to tackle the inequitable distribution of doctors in Thailand: Four decades of experience. *Human Resources for Health,* 1, 1–17.

Willen, S., Mulligan, J., & Castañeda, H. (2011). Take a stand commentary: How can medical anthropologists contribute to contemporary conversations on 'illegal' immigration and health? *Medical Anthropology Quarterly,* 25(3), 331–356.

Wright, T. (2007). *State terrorism in Latin America: Chile, Argentina, and international human rights.* Lanham, MD: Rowman & Littlefield.

INDEX

abortion 52
accreditation agencies 49
accreditation of medical facilities abroad 49, 85
addiction therapy 58
affective (im)mobilities 12, 32–34
affective labor (in caring for medical travelers) 118–121
anonymity, need for 43
Antigua, as destination for medical travel 58
'arenas of constraint' concept 107
Argentina: basic indicators of population and health 66; cancer treatment and the need to travel 67–69; care problems experienced by less privileged patients 117–118; centralized model of care delivery 10; current healthcare system 65–66; decentralized planning of healthcare provision 63–65; as destination for medical travel 58; discrimination felt by patients from outside the country 34; ethnographic research on pediatric medical travel 69–82; experience of medical travelers from Bolivia and Paraguay 97–98; factors shaping patients' experiences 109–111; families without formal support for medical travel 93; history of the healthcare system 59–65; lack of national cancer treatment protocols 67–69; *medicina prepaga* (prepaid medicine) companies 65; motivators of internal medical travel 100; *obras sociales* healthcare system 59, 63–65; pediatric oncology patients' access to healthcare 67–69; pediatric oncology services 40; populations viewed as 'deserving' or 'undeserving' 60; PROFE (federal health benefits program) 102–104, 106; ROHA registry of pediatric oncology patients 39; role of families and communities 90; sectors of the healthcare system 59; travel to Buenos Aires for cancer treatment 68–69; travel for pediatric oncology treatment 10
art and mobilities 27
ASEAN (Association of South-East Asian Nations) countries: healthcare delivery collaboration 40
aspiration for movement 32
assistance migration 6, 39
assisted reproductive technologies (ARTs) *see* fertility tourism/treatment; reproductive medical travel
assumptions of medical travel 44–48
availability of treatment or procedures 42–43

Bahamas, as destination for medical travel 58
Bangladesh, medical travelers from 40
Barbados, as destination for medical travel 58
barriers to medical travel 93–94
biomedical model 19
biomedical pilgrimage 6
bios (human experience) 55

INDEX

Bolivia, medical travel to Argentina from 34, 40, 58, 97–98
borders: conceptualizations of 28; types encountered by internal medical travelers 93
Brage, Eugenia 90, 110, 117
brain drain in destination healthcare systems 50–51
Brazil, as destination for medical travel 2, 58, 87

Canada, sending patients abroad from 41
capital, mobility as 31
cardiac procedures, cost of 40
Caribbean: impact of flows of medical travelers 59; medical travel destinations in 58–59
Carillo, Ramón 61–62
cases *see* ethnographic research on pediatric medical travel
challenges and risks of medical travel 48–53
choice, role of in medical care 98–100
class: influence on mobility 5; patterns of domination in science and medicine 18
commoditization of health and healthcare 21, 44, 45–47, 84–85
community members: role in facilitating medical travel 90
complications (medical), burden of absorbed by local hospitals 53
consumer choice in medical care 98–100
continuity of care issues 52–53
co-presence concept 30–31
cosmetic surgery 2, 40–41, 43, 58, 87, 88–89, 92, 116, 119
Costa Rica, as destination for medical travel 2, 58, 88–89, 92, 116, 119
country of origin preference 43–44
critical (im)mobilities framework: affective (im)mobilities 12, 32–34; affective journeys and the imagination 113–122; application to medical travel 4–5, 23–35; differential medical travel experiences and possibilities 95–111; differential mobility empowerments 11–12, 29–31; exploration of medical travel 10–11; imagined mobilities and possibilities 31–32; infrastructures of medical travel 11, 27–29, 84–94; mobilities paradigm 24–27; mobility as capital 29–31; overview 125–126; themes 11–12
critical ethics 4, 21–22
critical geography 4
critical medical anthropology (CMA) 4, 18–19
critical medical geography 19–21
critical perspectives 4; on medical travel 17–35
cross-border care 6, 40, 41
cultural hybridity of destination countries 47
cultural mobilities 27
culturally appropriate care 43
Czech Republic, as destination for medical travel 30, 89, 98, 110, 116, 118–119

dental treatment 40
destination countries: cultural hybridity 47; post-colonial political economy 22–23; re-working of cultural identity 22–23; strategic essentialism 47; *see also individual countries*
destination healthcare systems: creation of multiple-tiered healthcare systems 48, 51; domination of medical services by medical travelers 22; internal brain drain 50–51; negative impacts on 50–51; prioritization of specialized care over basic local needs 51
diasporic dreaming 115
discrimination 34
distributive justice 21
domination, patterns of 18
Dominican Republic, as destination for medical travel 58
Dubai, as destination for medical travel 101, 108, 110. 116

Eastern Europe, as destination for medical travel 2, 38
economic reasons for medical travel 42
egalitarian view of healthcare 21–22
embodied states 33–34
emotional dimension of travel: critical perspective 113–122; medical travel 12, 34; mobility and stasis 5, 32–34
emotional labor: caring for medical travelers 118–121
emotional toll on parents 121
ethical issues in medical travel 51–52; illegal treatments 51–52; stratified care 99–100; working-class patients used for surgeon training 87
ethics *see* critical ethics
ethnicity: influence on mobility 5; patterns of domination in science and medicine 18
ethnographic research: application to medical travel 8–9; definition 8; factors shaping patients' experiences 109–111; methods of studying mobilities 25–27
ethnographic research on pediatric medical travel 69–82; Adriana 102; Ana 104; Camila 78–80, 102, 106, 120; children and parents who shared their stories 74–76; Claudio 119; concluding thoughts 82; data analysis 72–74; data collection 70–72; Diego 110–111; Emiliano 104; Eulalia 2, 93; fieldwork 70–72; Jessica 104; Lucia 121; Marta 119, 121; Martin 117–118; Rodrigo 80–82, 117, 118, 120; Sebastian 76–78, 101, 102–103, 121; three stories of internal medical travel 76–82
European patients, medical travel destinations of 58, 92
European Union: regulation of medical travel websites 50
euthanasia 43, 52
experiences of medical travel, diversity of 95–111
experimental therapies 42–43, 52

facilitators of medical travel 88–89
families, role of in facilitating medical travel 90
family duties, medical travel and 119–121
fertility tourism/treatment 2, 42, 43–44, 52, 58, 97; *see also* reproductive medical travel
financial implications of medical travel 41, 100–104
'flat world' myth of global healthcare 44, 45–47
follow-up care: concerns about 52–53; patients' experiences of 109–111
Frankfurt School of critical theory 18
Fundación Eva Peron 61
funding of medical travel 41, 100–104
future areas of exploration 127–129; experiences of those accompanying medical travelers 129; failed attempts at medical travel 127; imagined journeys that never materialize 127; immobility concept 127; internal medical travel 128–129; logistics of medical travel 128

Geertz, Clifford 124
gender: influence on mobility 5; patterns of domination in science and medicine 18
gender reassignment surgery (GRS) 43, 91–92, 115
gendered mobilities 27
geographies of health 20
German medical travelers, destinations of 98, 116
global assemblage concept in medical travel 86
global infrastructures 84–86
global medical travel 37–55; intra-regional traffic 40; patient flows 39–41; reasons for travel 42–44; scale of 38–39
globalization: commoditization of healthcare 44, 45–47; influence on medical travel 38–39

INDEX

Habermas, Jürgen 18
hair loss therapy and transplants 58
health: representation as a commodity 21, 44, 45–47; representation as a human right 21
health insurance, financing of medical travel through 41
healthcare access: political nature of 18–19; unequal distribution of 21; uneven development of health services and 21
healthcare inequality *see* inequalities in healthcare
healthcare professionals: brain drain to private facilities 4; interface agent concept 108–110
hospitals, reconfiguration of in relation to people, time, and objects 29
human right, conceptualization of health as a 21

idealized notions of travel and care 114–116
illegal medical treatments: covert methods of delivery 91; means to circumvent regulations 98; medical travel to obtain 51–52, 91
imaginaries: definition 31–32; of medical travel and care 115–116
imagination: influence on experiences of travel 113–122; influence on mobility 5; motivator of medical travel 97–98; role in travel experiences 12
imagined futures, role of in medical travel decisions 114–116
imagined mobilities and possibilities 31–32
immobilities, critical perspective of 115–116
India: as destination for medical travel 40, 41, 42, 47, 49, 53; impacts on local healthcare costs 50, 51
inequalities in healthcare: capacity for mobility 4–5; critical perspective of 18; impact of medical travel on 3–4, 87; shedding light on 124; stratified care 99–100

information provided to medical travel patients 49–50
informed consent and risk communication 49–50
infrastructures: involvement in mobilities 27–29; sense of promise created by roads 33
infrastructures for medical travel 11, 83–94; barriers to medical travel 93–94; borders encountered by internal medical travelers 93–94; constant refiguring of 91–93; constrained journeys 94; creation of local infrastructures for care delivery 86–87; facilitators of medical travel 88–89; families without formal support 93; global infrastructures 84–86; 'hidden' and informal actors 89–91; impact on local healthcare delivery 87; ongoing infrastructuring process 91–93; online intermediaries 89; temporalities of 28–29
interface agent concept 108–110
international medical travel 38–39
intimate labor 118
intra-national medical travel 57–82; ethnographic research 10, 69–82; patient flows 41; scale of 39
intra-regional medical travel 38, 40
in-vitro fertilization (IVF) *see* fertility tourism/treatment; reproductive medical travel

Java: mobility dreams of village guides 33
journeys imagined but never enacted 98
justice, theories of 21–22

Korean patients, travel of to home country for treatment 44

landscapes: definition 20; perceptions and feelings associated with 20; therapeutic 20
Latin America, medical travel destinations in 58–59

INDEX

legality of treatments 42–43
liver transplant, cost of 40
local economic growth, belief that medical travel contributes to 44–45, 47–48
local healthcare: belief that medical travel will improve it 44–45, 47–48; impact of medical travel 87
local travel *see* intra-national medical travel
logistics of medical travel 100–104

Malaysia: as destination for medical travel 23, 39, 40, 47, 53; internal brain drain 51; use of public facilities by private patients 51
malpractice law: variations between countries 53
medical exiles 6
medical facilities and practitioners: arenas of constraint 107; creation of a home away from home 116–118; interactions with 107–111
medical geography 19–21
medical refugees 6
medical tourism 21, 92, 96; definition and connotations 5–6
medical travel: complexity and difficulties faced by patients 6; definition 2; destinations in Latin America and the Caribbean 58–59; diversity of practices and experiences 95–111; healthcare inequality and 3–4; impact on quality of local healthcare 3–4; number of people travelling abroad each year 2; reasons for 2; scope of the concept 6–7; terminology used for 5–6; theories of justice and 21–22; value of the global industry 3
medical travel agencies, discourse used by 89
medical travel broker websites 49–50
medical travel facilitators 88–89
medical travel flows 39–41

medical travel industry: appropriation and domination of local medical services 22; commoditization of health 84–85; regulation and monitoring issues 85
medical travel infrastructures *see* infrastructures for medical travel
medical travel market: influence of online communities 92
medical travel possibilities 97–98
medical travelers, hardships endured by to access medical resources 92–93
medicine: patterns of ideological domination 18
methodological approaches: overview 125–126
Mexico, as destination for medical travel 38, 40, 41, 58, 88
migrants: emotional dimension of moving 32; undocumented migrants' access to health services 28
mobilities: differential empowerments 11–12, 29–31; incomplete 32; limitations on some people 3; power relations and 11–12; range of reasons for travel 7; range of journey types 7; research methods 25–27; that are never enacted 32
mobilities paradigm 4–5, 24–27
mobilities turn in the social sciences 4, 24–27
mobility capital 31
mobility/immobility continuum 25
moral issues in medical travel 22
motility 12, 32
movement: factors which allow or hinder movement 25; power asymmetries and 4–5; reshaping of people, things, and ideas 24–25
'myths' of medical travel 44–48

neocolonialism, medical travel as a form of 22–23
neoliberal view of the patient-consumer 45, 48
network capital, mobility as 31

non-biomedical treatments 120
North American patients: medical travel destinations of 38–43, 58, 88, 92, 118–119; patient-consumers 45, 48

online communities, influence of on the medical travel market 92
online intermediaries for medical travel 89
Ormond, Meghan 23, 46, 47, 51, 85

Paraguay, medical travel to Argentina from 34, 40, 58, 97–98
parents: emotional toll of fighting for care for their child 119–121; record-keeping 121
patient: definition of the term 7
patient-consumer activism 89
patient-consumer view 6, 45, 48, 84–85; choice in medical care 98–100
patient flows 39–41
patients: complexity and difficulties of medical travel 6; influence of online communities 92; online support groups and blogs 89; symbolic dimensions of medical travel 12
pediatric oncology patients: access to healthcare 67–69; travel within Argentina 10; *see also* ethnographic research on pediatric medical travel
Peron, Eva 61
place: application to access to healthcare 20; definition 20; ideas and perceptions of 20
post-colonial theory 4, 22–23
post-medical geography of health 20
potential journeys 115
potential mobility 12, 32
power, expressed through infrastructures 27–29
power differentials: critical (im)mobilities approach 27; influence on access to healthcare 18–19; influence on mobility 29–31; movement and 4–5; stratified care and 99–100
prioritarian view of healthcare 21

privacy, need for 43
privilege: critical (im)mobilities approach 27
process of traveling 105–107
prostate cancer surgery 58
public facilities, use of by private patients 51

quality of care, concerns about 52–53

regulation of medical travel facilities 48–49, 85
reproductive medical travel 30, 43–44, 86, 89, 90, 97, 98, 101, 108, 110, 114–116, 118–119; *see also* fertility tourism/treatment
research on medical travel: anthropological studies 54; areas of strength 126; descriptive studies 53; empirical focus 8, 53–54; epistemological openness and invigoration 129–130; ethnographic research 8–9; ethnographic research on pediatric medical travel 69–82; future areas of exploration 127–129; future directions 55; intra-national medical travel studies 10; methods of studying mobilities 25–27; political and economic perspectives 54–55; rights perspective 54–55; stages of development 53–55; studies 8–10; theoretical perspectives 54
return migration 6, 97
rights to health services: categories of citizens 54–55
risk communication and informed consent 49–50
risks of medical travel 48–53
rogue medical tourism 90

science: patterns of ideological domination 18
selective essentialism 23
Singapore, as destination for medical travel 39, 53
social sciences: mobilities turn 4, 24–27

Spain, as destination for medical travel 98, 116
spinal surgery 58
stasis: relationship to mobility 25
state power, expressed through infrastructures 27–29
status quo: questioning and critical analysis 27
stem cell therapies 42–43, 52
strategic essentialism 47
stratified care, power asymmetries and 99–100
sufficientarian view of healthcare 22
symbolic dimensions of travel: critical perspective 113–122; medical travel 12; mobility and stasis 32–34

telemedicine 110
Thailand: creation of a two-tier healthcare system 51; destination for medical travel 38, 39, 40, 41, 42, 47, 53, 86–87, 91–92, 115; internal brain drain 50–51

theoretical approaches: overview 125–126
therapeutic landscapes 20
travelers, creation of categories of 28
treatment costs, as reason for medical travel 42

UK: sending patients abroad from 41; waiting times for treatments 42
US *see* North American patients
utilitarian view of healthcare 21

waiting times, as reason for medical travel 42

Yemeni patients: decision to go abroad for treatment 119; journeys imagined by patients 97; social sharing of medical travel stories 90

zoe (bare life) 55

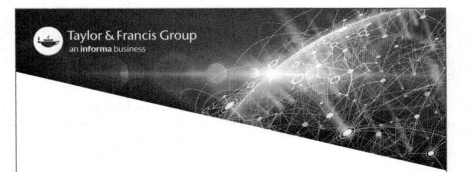